Wrestling with Giants

Also by John Young

The Case Against Christ (Hodder & Stoughton)
Creating Confidence in Evangelism (CPAS)
Explore Your Faith (Hodder & Stoughton)
Jesus: The Verdict (Lion)
Know Your Faith (Hodder & Stoughton)
Practical Ideas in Evangelism (CPAS)
Teach Yourself Christianity (Hodder & Stoughton)

Wrestling with Giants

Stories of Hope and Faith
for all who Struggle

Edited by John Young

Hodder & Stoughton
LONDON SYDNEY AUCKLAND

To Felix from Japan and Janet from York,
and all others who wrestle with giants
and inspire others.

Copyright © 2000 John Young

First published in Great Britain in 2000

The right of John Young to be identified as the Editor of
the Work has been asserted by him in accordance with
the Copyright, Designs and Patents Act 1988.

10 9 8 7 6 5 4 3 2 1

British Library Cataloguing in Publication Data
A record for this book is available from the British Library

ISBN 0 340 75681 0

Typeset by Avon Dataset Ltd, Bidford-on-Avon, Warks

Printed and bound in Great Britain by
Clays Ltd, St Ives plc

Hodder & Stoughton
A Division of Hodder Headline Limited
338 Euston Road
London NW1 3BH

Contents

Thank you

I am tremendously grateful to Barrie and Joan Stephenson, Walter and Pauline Stockdale, Max Wigley and Chris Woodcock for allowing us to step inside their lives and to share their experiences. It has been a great privilege to work with them on this book.

But thanks are due to others too, especially to David Moloney, the Commissioning Editor at Hodder and Stoughton, who is so committed to providing books which are a resource for living in the 'real' world.

As always, I am also indebted to my colleague Simon Stanley, who conducted the interviews and made the tape recordings on which these five chapters are based. The audio-tape interviews are available from *York Courses* to those who wish to listen to the contributors, as well as to read their stories (see page 3).

Finally, I wish to thank Helena Rogers who took those audio tapes and transformed them into words on paper. She did most of the hard work and my co-contributors join me in expressing our warm gratitude to Helena.

John Young
York

A damaged hip

The most famous wrestling match in history is recorded in the Bible (Genesis 32:22–31). As Jacob wrestled with God throughout the night, he wrestled with other giants too – with his past, with his sense of identity, and with his need for forgiveness and renewal. Jacob was changed and God gave him a new name to mark this transformation. This name has travelled down the centuries and lives today. Israel.

Jacob did not come through this fierce struggle without injury. His hip was damaged and he limped for the rest of his journey.

The word 'wrestle' is also used in a famous New Testament passage. The apostle Paul tells us that we wrestle ('struggle' in some translations) not with flesh and blood but with 'the spiritual forces of evil in the heavenly realms' (Ephesians 6:12).

The word itself is not used much elsewhere in the Scriptures (my concordance gives just two other references) but the idea is central.

Peter wrestled with a deep sense of guilt and failure, following his denial of Christ. Paul struggled with his 'thorn in the flesh' (2 Corinthians:12:7–9). In the wilderness, Jesus wrestled with the meaning of his vocation and the shape of his ministry. And in the Garden of Gethsemane he wrestled with a deep sense of dread.

When Jesus calls people to follow him, he makes wonderful promises. But along with the 'homes, brothers, sisters . . . and eternal life' (Mark 10:30) there is one other tell-tale word: 'persecutions'.

Jesus is a realist. He never promises his followers an easy ride through life. But he does promise to be with us day in, day out, adding joy to the good times and bringing strength and encouragement in difficult times.

This is the experience of the contributors to this book. Every one of them has wrestled with a giant – in some cases more than one. They share their experiences with us, not to provide a blue-print for coping with suffering, but to give us a glimpse into their struggles and the lessons they have learned along the way. In particular, we are privileged to share the way in which their Christian faith has proved to be a vital resource. Their openness and honesty is moving and sometimes inspiring.

The giants described in this book roam our world today.

They are restless, ugly, fierce and tenacious. They are not easily defeated and – like Jacob – wrestling with them usually changes us. Sometimes the struggle leaves us damaged too.

Panic attacks, bereavement, cancer, depression and the shock of discovering that a first child has severe disabilities, are found in every street. Millions of people wrestle with these giants. The contributors to this book hope that it will find its way into many homes. And they pray that their stories will help others who 'wrestle with giants'.

Four conversations on which this book is based are recorded on two audio tapes. See page 117 for further details.

STRUGGLING/COPING?

Tape 1 – Side A –   Living with panic attacks
                    (Max Wigley)

        – Side B –   Living with depression
                    (John Young)

Tape 2 – Side A –   Living with cancer
                    (Walter and Pauline Stockdale)

        – Side B –   Living with bereavement
                    (Chris Woodcock)

1

Living with panic attacks: Max's story

Max Wigley was born in Selby, Yorkshire, and has lived in Yorkshire most of his life. He worked for ICI in Harrogate for five years before training for the Anglican ministry in London. After five years as a curate on Merseyside he became a vicar in Bradford in 1969, and has since served in Pudsey and his current parish in Yeadon.

He is married to Judith and has four children, a daughter in Buckingham, a son in Bangkok, and twins, a boy and a girl, aged eighteen years. He has three grandchildren. His main interest is sport, having played both cricket and soccer into his forties. He now plays golf – badly!

Standing before the fourteen-storey block of flats in Liverpool, it occurred to me that I had not anticipated this particular problem. I had looked forward to beginning my work as a curate with both excitement and apprehension. I had no illusions about the challenging nature of the appointment, but standing at the entrance to the high-rise block I was taken by surprise. I thought I'd prepared myself for most things, but I had missed this one. For – inevitably – I needed to get to the top floor of the block. There were two ways of achieving this end: one was to walk up the twenty-eight flights of stairs, the other was to take the lift. But I hated lifts!

Suddenly the fear I had always had of lifts triggered the familiar adrenaline surge I had come to recognise. It hit me in the chest and spread instantly right out to my fingers and toes, making my legs weak. My hands went cold, and yet beads of perspiration broke out on my forehead. Instinctively I wanted to turn and run – to get as far as possible from that lift, in the shortest time.

I had always been susceptible to panic attacks. From childhood the urge to 'cut and run' had affected me in varying situations. I could not always tell when this was going to happen, and particularly as a child I didn't have experience to call upon. Sometimes the occasion itself would cause panic – like the time I took my eleven-plus examination.

In those days – 1948, in my case – a child's entire life seemed to hang on the successful outcome – or not – of the eleven-plus exam. Pass it, and you found yourself eligible for a grammar school and a subsequent 'good job'. Fail it, and you were sent to the secondary modern school with the rest of the 'failures', to make out as best you could. I am not aware that my parents pressurised me unduly, so I don't think they were to blame entirely – although my father made me aware of how important passing the exam was for my future. He'd been deprived of the opportunity because his parents couldn't afford for him to go to grammar school. They needed his wage packet. So I certainly felt the weight of the occasion.

Clutching my pencil case, I walked into the imposing hall with unfamiliar children and unknown staff. Then I was presented with the examination paper on which my future was to be decided. This proved exactly the occasion for the onset of a panic attack. Needless to say, I failed the examination.

However, I spent only one year at the secondary modern school. At the age of twelve I was transferred to a junior technical college and then, at fifteen, to a grammar school in Knaresborough. The grammar school experience continued the pattern I had, by now, come to expect. I arrived in the middle of a year and had to start from scratch to catch up and become accepted in already established groups. It was not, therefore, a particularly happy time for me, although the few years at the technical college had proved a respite from my life of change.

For no apparent reason, at the junior technical college I found myself on a two-year building course. I imagine a teacher with a keen sense of humour recommended me for this since I am hopeless at manual work – a DIY disaster area! However, I actually enjoyed the course, because for the first time I started at the same time as all the other kids. Up until then, my education had consisted of being moved from place to place, school to school, thanks to my father's job in the police force. This, I believe, is where the root of my insecurities, and consequent panic attack problem, may well lie.

I began my school life at the age of four in 1942. Being considered 'bright', I was soon moved into the class of five-year-olds. Classes were arranged very differently in those days. The most able children sat in state at one end of the room. The rest were seated strictly in order of ability up and down the rows to the far side of the room, where all the 'dumdums' were deposited. There could be no mistake, therefore, about your standing among your peers. You – and everyone else – *knew* if you were failing.

Having been sent up a class halfway through a year, I found myself counted with the 'dumdums'. I didn't know the other children because my friends were all four-year-olds – a year made an enormous difference at that age – and neither did I know what lessons they were doing. I felt totally and utterly lost and desolate. Other children may have coped with this situation better than I did, but my nature and personality found the arrangement very difficult to handle. Perhaps this formed the basis of my propensity to panic attacks.

The continual moving from school to school certainly had a bearing on the situation. Most kids begin a new school or term together, often as a group of friends. In my case, I frequently found myself in situations where I was the only new child in the class, with everyone else well into the coursework. Usually, the teacher couldn't spare the time to bring me up to date with the work. So I remained confused and stumbled along until such time as I could catch up for myself. In any case, to be picked out for special attention by the teacher would bring its own form of stress. In addition to all this, I often could not do the homework we were given because of my lack of groundwork, so I struggled at home, too. All this went to reinforce the inevitable feeling that I was an outsider, both in work and friendships. I desperately needed to be accepted and that meant breaking into established groups of friends – but to be accepted I needed to succeed.

I particularly remember going to bed one night and starting to panic. I was too young to put my feelings into words, as unknown fears welled up inside me. I know now that they all concerned my acceptance in a stressful world. Would I ever be able to cope? Would the others ever accept me? Would I fail miserably? Would I be able to do the work? I had no answers. Darkness and panic swept over me. This pattern was repeated over the years and even into adulthood.

But a fear of failure was not the only fear that overcame me at these times. A fear of punishment also played a part. As I grew older I realised that it was an irrational fear, but it probably had its roots in my childhood experiences at junior school in Rotherham.

The head of this school considered himself something of an expert in maths and liked to pick out three or four pupils at a time to coach in his study. He was a bully and the prospect was terrifying for us seven- to eight-year-olds. No doubt he, too, was a product of his own past, but he bullied us, his pupils, unmercifully.

He would come into the class and pick out his victims for the session in his lair. We were terrified and dreaded seeing him enter our classroom. I, especially, tried to avoid the piercing gaze by hiding under my desk so that he wouldn't pick me! From time to time, however, in spite of my evasive efforts, I was marched along with the other poor unfortunates to the forbidding study. Once there, we were desperate to give the right answers to his questions, for if we got it wrong he would cane us there and then on both hands. I would be in such a state of fear that even if he had asked me what one and one added up to, I'm sure I would have got it wrong! The whole experience bred a need to achieve or be punished. My formative mind retained that warped lesson to plague me with for the rest of my life.

Years later, when I was struggling with anxiety and near panic in a difficult new parish situation, a friend challenged me. 'Who's sitting on your shoulder?' he said. 'Who's egging you on to achieve or be punished?' He was right, of course. As I thought about it, I realised that although punishment had a part to play in my panic feelings, I had no reason to feel that way. No one was going to punish me for getting anything wrong any more. It was simply a vestige of my past. The knowledge didn't eliminate the fear of not achieving, not being accepted and the subsequent near panic. But it added a little more to my understanding of the reasons behind my reactions, and this insight helped my efforts to control them.

Of course, during my childhood I had no idea why these disturbing panic attacks happened. They simply reinforced my feelings of isolation and of being 'different' from most of the other kids who had – or appeared to have – 'ordinary', settled lives. As a teenager, however, something happened which altered the whole emphasis of my life and gave me a completely different view of everything – including my panic attacks.

As a child I had always been involved in church life, albeit on a nominal level. I was a member of the choir, and I believed in God. I also enjoyed the social structure which provided various activities to take part in and friends to share them with. One evening in 1955 I went to see a Christian film at the Lounge Hall in Harrogate, called *Oil Town USA*. That a Christian organisation should become involved in film production at a professional level was unheard of in those days, but as a follow-up to the Harringay Crusades, these films were being shown across the country. Billy Graham had brought his vast crusades to Britain early in the 1950s, and many people had responded to the appeal at the end of the meetings to 'come down to the front' and commit their lives to Christ. Similarly, the film attracted many thousands and, as usual, an appeal was given at the end of the film. I responded.

Gradually the Church and its teaching began to make sense. It focused finally and vividly on Jesus Christ and what he had done for me. I had no option but to respond to the invitation. From that time on, with all my imperfections, my life centred on God and my aims and aspiration slowly changed.

On leaving school I had worked as a lab technician for ICI, taking day-release to work for my HNC. But now this all seemed somehow 'off-centre'. My attention veered towards the Church and I began to wonder if God was calling me to be ordained as a clergyman in the Church of England. It took just a few years to convince me that this was indeed how God wanted me to serve him. Eventually I took steps to acquire the appropriate qualifications.

I spent a pre-theological college year with the Bernard Gilpin Society in Durham and then entered Oak Hill College, London, to study for my ordination examinations. After completing my studies I prepared for ordination at Chester Cathedral in 1964. All ordinands were required to undertake an ordination retreat when we were expected to remain secluded and quiet, spending the time in Bible study, prayer and communion with God. I viewed the approaching three days with increasing anxiety. To begin with, I hated being separated from people. I functioned best when with others and I didn't find it easy being on my own.

Years later I attended a course as part of my in-service training which provided me with some explanation of my unease. It came via an assessment of personality types based on the Myers–Briggs test. I discovered that I fitted into the 'E' – 'Extravert' – category, but with the sub-division category of 'S' for 'Sensing'. I am undoubtedly an 'out-there' sort of person – energised by people and what goes on in the outside world, and directing my energy outwards. But I also tend to be a 'Sensing' person – one who tends to focus on the present and on concrete information gained from the senses. At the other end of the scale is the person who focuses on the future in the light of patterns and possibilities.

All this fitted with the way I reacted to all sorts of situations. I recalled the times when I had been excited by something in a meeting with my staff, when we had decided on some plan or other. I would rush to tell my wife. 'This is great!' I would enthuse, 'I'm gonna do this right now!'

Then, in accordance with her personality type (she's the opposite to me!), she would bring me back to earth, saying, 'Yes – but what will the outcome be in six months' time? Have you thought it through adequately?'

Being an 'Extravert' and mainly energised by people, I don't function well when left to my own devices. It therefore came as something of a problem to me when my ordination retreat insisted that I spend three days alone in silence. I really hate being quiet and alone, and, with time to think about the future and possible failure, I found the old fears and panic welling up even at the thought of the isolation. This, in turn, led to guilt feelings about not being spiritual enough – especially when many of the other ordinands seemed to enjoy the quiet times. Every so often we had a 'quiet day' at college: many of the men would

13

say, 'Wonderful! A day of peace and quiet!' and I would silently think, 'Oh, no! I'm going to hate this.' At the time this was the worst thing that could happen to me. I had a real struggle on that ordination retreat as I looked into the future with illogical feelings and fears.

But now that I had discovered my personality type, I also discovered why I had these feelings. I didn't have to try and 'snap out of' them. There was nothing wrong with me. My fears and attitudes were a result of the way God made me and the experiences of my early years. We all experience formative situations which can be either positive or negative. We live in a fallen world, so we are scarred by the negative experiences we have in it. The mind is an amazing and complicated thing. It is affected by all these experiences, and we have to live with them as best we can. Even the most insignificant incident can trigger something from the past.

For instance, I recently met a woman who lives almost next door to my mother. To my astonishment, I discovered that not only was she exactly my age, but that we were in the same class at grammar school! I hadn't recognised her. She brought out old photographs of some of the kids we knew – kids I hadn't seen for forty years – and it all came back just as though it were yesterday! The wonderful computer that is our brain brought it all back again. Our minds are full of memories, some of which cause scars. We can't always bring them to the front – and neither should we try, necessarily – but they do affect the way we react in different situations.

As a pastor and evangelist I have been aware that every human condition and emotion is mirrored in the pages of the Bible. God has revealed everything we need to know in order to assist us on our Christian journey. So it comes as no surprise to discover that people in the Bible have suffered all kinds of emotional traumas – depression and panic attacks, in particular, figuring vividly. It would seem that these debilitating conditions have been around for a long time. They have hampered the great men of God in much the same way as they hamper me. Our Principal at Theological College first drew my attention to examples of people who suffer in this kind of pit.

'Look in the psalms,' he said, 'they are full of people who are going through the valleys and the dark times, when things just overwhelm them.'

I looked and saw a kaleidoscope of human experience. Written there were examples of people who are probably panicking, depressed, fearful – depression being a forerunner, or at least an ally, of panic attacks. Gradually I realised that all this is part of human nature. But even more important and wonderful is the fact that although we walk through the darkest valley, God is in it with us – even though we might not *feel* as though he's there. Thousands of Christians with outstanding ministries have felt this way.

However, at the same time I had to contend with the branch of theology that says, 'Oh well, if you had enough faith, you wouldn't have this sort of problem.' In the first place, people who say this have no understanding of what panic attacks and depression really are. They think of them as simply an attitude of mind – something that can be 'snapped out of' – spiritual weakness. This is dangerously false. Illnesses don't consist only of visible symptoms like having spots when you catch measles, or a pot on your leg if you have a broken bone.

Panic attacks, fear and depression, are a sign of something inside. As I discovered, they may be brought on by childhood experiences. They have a definite cause and are nothing to feel guilty about. In the same way that we can ask God to be our strength and help when we are going through any other kind of illness, so we can ask God to help heal the scars that cause us to react emotionally in an irrational way.

Those who would tell us that Christians shouldn't have irrational fears are compounding the problem in another way. Not only does this makes us feel guilty, it can also undermine our faith. In fact, that attitude insinuates that faith is something you have to achieve, when it is actually a gift from God. I struggled with this until I read a definition of faith that I found quite liberating. It said, 'Faith is an affirmation of truth which results in obedience *despite* your feelings.' Faith is not something that we can work at to improve. Jesus said, 'I tell you the truth, if you have faith as small as a mustard seed, you can say to this mountain, "Move from here to there" and it will move. Nothing will be impossible to you' (Matthew 17:20).

I remember an old lady once coming to the communion

rail for laying on of hands at a healing service. She said, 'If only I had enough faith . . .'

'You had enough faith to walk up this aisle and kneel at these rails,' I answered. Her faith, even though small as a grain of mustard seed, resulted in her obedience to stumble forward. This is all God looks for – just a grain of mustard seed. If he wanted more than this, how would we ever know when we had reached the right level of faith? When could we know we had enough faith for God to say, 'Right, now I can do something for you'?

This smacks of a god who is not the God I see in Jesus Christ. That god is sitting 'up there' testing you and seeing whether you've achieved enough faith for something to happen. So if you are a person who gets depressed very easily or gets panic attacks, or whatever else it might be, you will not feel very much 'in tune' with God. You will probably be unable to feel his presence. Does this mean, then, that you have no chance of having your prayers answered? Nothing could be further from the truth. The God whom Jesus Christ portrayed is the God who accepts us with our small doubting, mustard-seed faith.

As all these conflicting thoughts went through my mind, I remembered the man in the Bible who came to Jesus, bringing his son who suffered from epilepsy (Matthew 17:14–20).

'If you can do anything,' said the man, 'take pity on us and help us.'

'*If* you can?' repeated Jesus. 'Everything is possible for him who believes.'

'I *do* believe,' exclaimed the man. 'Help me overcome my unbelief!'

What this man regarded as unbelief was in fact a doubting faith. It might have been as small as a grain of mustard seed, but it was real. This was demonstrated by the fact that he brought his son to Jesus. Jesus healed the son, so he obviously regarded the man's 'doubting faith' not as 'unbelief' but as saving faith.

We are sometimes like that. We tend to think that God demands a certain level of faith before he can do anything. Instead, he says, 'You come to me, with your doubting and stumbling faith as small as a grain of mustard seed, and leave the rest to me.'

During my work as a pastor and an evangelist presenting Christ to seeking enquirers, I have come up against this problem of people thinking that they don't have enough faith to believe.

'I *want* to believe, but I don't know if I have enough faith,' they say. 'I've had no religious background. I don't know anything about God.' They think they have to undergo some time of apprenticeship in order to reach a point where they can be acceptable to God!

I had the pleasure and privilege of presenting Christ to the famous comedian Bobby Ball, of 'Cannon and Ball'. He too was puzzled and doubting at first. But all it needed was one small step towards God – the mustard-seed faith – and God did the rest by reaching out to him as he has to many others.

Having said all this, the amount of faith we possess is

not a guarantee of healing. God has not, so far, healed me completely of my tendency to panic attacks – and yet my faith remains as strong as ever. Learning more about why I have them has enabled me to cope with them more easily, but I have not received full healing. Neither did Paul receive healing from his 'thorn in the flesh' (2 Corinthians 12:7). God uses our weakness to help us become more mature as Christians.

A life committed to God must accept his perfect will in all things. I have learned to accept the fact that I have occasional panic attacks. I do get anxious and depressed at times but, with God's help, I can make some attempt at controlling them. There is a verse in Hebrews that has always been a help to me. It says, 'Keep walking on straight paths so that the lame foot may not be disabled but instead be healed' (Hebrews 12:13, GNB). Our healing may not come completely until we move into eternity, but I think that if we move with him, and walk his 'straight path', the 'lame foot' begins to get easier, and the limp less pronounced.

I still get very fearful of an attack. The adrenaline surges through me and I want to turn and run – if only my legs would take me! I try to rationalise the situation by telling myself it is simply a 'fear of fear'. I insist that my fears are quite irrational – I have no reason to be afraid. I battle with my mind – and this is what I continue to do. I tell myself, 'There is no logical reason for me to be panicking in this way.' The attacks do still come sometimes, but as the years go by I am learning, with God's help, to cope with them.

One way in which I cope with them is to take evasive action in the form of some kind of sport. I channel my fears and energy into physical exercise. It takes my mind from the fear and changes the thought patterns that would otherwise dwell on the attack. In that way, whenever possible, I refuse to allow my mind to make more of the fear. I deliberately 'switch off' the fear-inducing adrenaline and, instead, channel it into something I enjoy. This breaks the pattern and reduces the likelihood of future attacks.

The worst thing possible is to focus on the panic and allow it full rein to build up and take control. When this happens, the fears become disabling and can restrict one from enjoying a full life. I am a fighter and competitor. I refuse to let this happen. I make every effort to face the fear and overcome it.

Some time ago I had the opportunity to visit our eldest son, who lives in Bangkok. As my wife was not able to take advantage of the opportunity, it meant that I would have to travel alone. I didn't fancy that. I had either to beat this huge hurdle or to give in and forgo the visit. The adrenaline began to surge as I considered the prospect. It would entail a long time on an aircraft – in itself a somewhat claustrophobic experience. I didn't dwell on the 'downside' of the journey. I told myself, 'I *will* do it!' – and I did! These things have to be fought. I refused to allow fear to deny me that wonderful opportunity.

More recently I also spent five weeks at St George's College in Jerusalem. I was really looking forward to the experience but was fearful of going alone. Again, I said, 'I'm gonna do this. I'll fight the fear and not let it get the better of me.' I had to fight or flee – and I chose to fight. If you want to do these things, you have to face the fear and fight it. Other people have no choice but to struggle with all kinds of trauma. It just isn't possible to give in and walk away from some things. My mind went to the many refugees who are going through horrific situations all over the world. Throughout their lives, they will suffer terrible trauma because of their experiences, but they've got to keep going. They may want to turn and run away, but they can't. My fears seem trivial in comparison – even though they are very real to me.

How could I give in to them when others suffer more? I must keep going too. But I can pray each time I have to overcome my fears. 'Lord, help me to win over this,' I ask, simply. God may not remove the panic attacks completely, but he does say, 'I am with you always' (Matthew 28:20). He is with us whether we ask him or not. He is with us on the mountains and in the valleys. 'I can do everything through him who gives me strength,' said Paul (Philippians 4:13).

Maybe I am still allowed to experience the panic attacks sometimes, because God knows that I will function best in his service while having to struggle with this problem. 'My power is made perfect in weakness,' God tells us in Corinthians (2 Corinthians 12:9). We can never be effective in our own strength. We need to rely on God's strength only. If we think we are capable of succeeding on our own, then we don't need God's help. We lean on him all the more in our weakness.

I have never felt that my service for God has been restricted because of my panic attacks. I suppose that if I had given in to the problem and refused to take on the opportunities God sent, then I would now be a slave to fear. I could never let that happen. I have fought the problem all the way – relying on God's help every time. I may not always have won all the battles, but making an effort to overcome them is vital and makes the next attack just that little bit easier to control.

I took one step on the long road of struggle as I stood before that block of flats in Liverpool. Fourteen storeys! Well, there was no way I would be walking up twenty-eight flights of stairs. It had to be the lift. I took a deep breath, stepped forward and pressed the lift call button . . .

WORDS OF HOPE AND FAITH

One night, during a particularly stressful time in my life, I was tossing and turning in bed, unable to sleep. But as I was half-asleep a verse came into my mind from nowhere. It was something to do with not being afraid of the terror of the night nor the arrow that flies by day. I had no idea where it came from. And then, into my subconscious mind came the words 'Psalm 91'. At that point I felt a peace and dropped into a fitful sleep. As soon as I woke up I asked Judith to pass me my Bible, which I opened at Psalm 91. It was as if God had penned it for me and I knew it was his word for me at that time. That was twenty years ago and I still remember it as yesterday.

Psalm 91

He who dwells in the shelter of the Most High
  will rest in the shadow of the Almighty.
I will say of the LORD, 'He is my refuge and my fortress,
  my God, in whom I trust.'
Surely he will save you from the fowler's snare
  and from the deadly pestilence.
He will cover you with his feathers,
  and under his wings you will find refuge;
  his faithfulness will be your shield and rampart.
You will not fear the terror of night,
  nor the arrow that flies by day,
nor the pestilence that stalks in the darkness,
  nor the plague that destroys at midday.

A thousand may fall at your side,
  ten thousand at your right hand,
  but it will not come near you.
You will only observe with your eyes
  and see the punishment of the wicked.
If you make the Most High your dwelling –
  even the LORD, who is my refuge –
then no harm will befall you,
  no disaster will come near your tent.
For he will command his angels concerning you
  to guard you in all your ways;
they will lift you up in their hands,
  so that you will not strike your foot against a stone.
You will tread upon the lion and the cobra;
  you will trample the great lion and the serpent.
'Because he loves me,' says the LORD, 'I will rescue him;
  I will protect him, for he acknowledges my name.
He will call upon me, and I will answer him;
  I will be with him in trouble,
  I will deliver him and honour him.
With long life will I satisfy him
  and show him my salvation.'

A book which I have found extremely helpful is *Free to Fail*, by Russ Parker. It helped me to realise that many of the prophets in the Bible were called to tasks for which the result would be failure. For example, Jeremiah failed to turn his people away from their sin and suffered terribly himself. When Isaiah was called (in Isaiah 6) he responded, but was told that his people would take no notice of his message.

The way of the cross was a way of failure: rejection, slander, misunderstanding and finally death for our Lord. In the eyes of the people, the Romans and the Jewish leaders, he was a failure. Possibly even in the eyes of the disciples.

We are called to walk that way too. Christ was not delivered *from* the cross – he was delivered *on* it. That truth has always encouraged me. We are called to walk the way of the cross, often to suffer, and even to be 'failures'.

Sheila Cassidy in her book *Good Friday People* mentions those people in particular who are very specially loved by God because he has called them to walk towards him along a certain narrow path – the road to Calvary. It is of course the same road taken by the Son of God as he went on his journey of life and death. There is no romance or nostalgia on this Calvary road, for it is the way of loss and suffering. Cassidy goes on to identify two results of this journey. Some of the walkers are purified and strengthened and go on to do great things for God. The others are quite simply broken, stripped bare and destroyed. Christ, it seems – and this is our ultimate healing – embraces both results. So it is that Jesus calls us to take up our cross and to follow him. In doing so, he reminds us that the cross is not some temporary spiritual dark night of the soul which, once endured, leads us on into better times of success and maturity; the cross is a continuous experience of living with suffering and failure. Dom Dominic Gaisford wrote that it is in this sense that Christianity is a religion of failure, whereas we want and expect it to be a recipe for living our lives happily and contentedly. What Gaisford is underlining is the need to stay vulnerable and open to life in the raw, rather than using Christianity as some form of escapism into a 'happy ever after' story more familiar in fairy tales than in true gospel living. According to Gaisford it is this demand to stay vulnerable that is implicit in facing the cross. Jesus, in his earthly life, refused to dodge the call of the cross for an easy life of unstoppable power. He suffered all the dissatisfactions of being misunderstood and misjudged by friends, family and enemies alike. 'His was an unrequited love on a massive scale that must have amounted to an almost intolerable experience for him of loneliness and failure.' Yet Jesus is not wishing to deny moments of power; but he does bring them all into the focus of the greater reality of the cross, the Calvary lifestyle.

Luke, in his Gospel, points up the contrast of Jesus going from the mountain-top experience to the ignominy of the cross. Jesus sits on the Mount of Transfiguration with the great saints of the Old Testament period, Moses and Elijah. His disciples sit in awe as they see something of Christ's majesty shine through his face. Before the chapter is completed Jesus has 'resolutely set out for Jerusalem' (9:51). The passage implies that there were many distractions or high moments that Jesus could have held on to, but no, he had to go to Jerusalem and embrace his cross. Jesus never lost sight of the importance of the cross which lay before him and to this end he would even burst in on the joy of his disciples and endeavour to prepare them for what was to come both for himself and them (cf. Matt. 16:16ff.).

At apparently the peak of success, Jesus talks about the cross. He is saying that the focus for Christian power as well as for suffering has to be the fact and event of his cross. Everything in the disciples' experience must align itself with this significant moment of Calvary. Every success must be brought to his cross; every issue of suffering, whether it leads to insight or is stuck in pain, must be brought to the cross. We cannot explain completely why God asks this of us, but surely it is primarily because at Calvary God demonstrates most powerfully, and in the greatest weakness, his abiding presence in times of overcoming and times of suffering. Both triumph and torture are brought to balance at this place where God chooses to be weak for our salvation.

From *Free to Fail* by Russ Parker (SPCK, 1992)

FOR REFLECTION . . .

1   Have you ever experienced the kind of panic which Max describes on page 6? If so, what triggered *your* strong desire to cut and run?

2   Do you suffer from panic attacks, or do you know people who do?

3   Do you feel it is helpful to look back at your childhood in an attempt to understand your adult reactions and responses? Or is it best to 'leave well alone' and concentrate on coping strategies for the present day?

4   Are you helped by the title *Free to Fail*, and the paragraphs chosen by Max to close his chapter?

5   Are you surprised that such an outgoing, 'up-front' Christian as Max suffers from panic attacks? What you do make of that?

2

Living with disability:
Barrie and Joan's story

Barrie and Joan Stephenson have three sons. They have lived in North Yorkshire all their married life. Their story starts while they are in a Pentecostal church. They spent ten years leading a Christian fellowship in Harrogate before moving to York and joining St Michael-le-Belfrey. Barrie is now the Managing Editor of BBC Radio York and Joan is a history teacher and year head at a secondary school in the city. Warwick now lives in his own house with four other adults with learning disabilities.

Just like any young couple, we looked forward eagerly to the birth of our first child. We wondered what he or she would be like; we occasionally indulged in a little specula-tion about his or her future and we sometimes felt perhaps a little inadequate for the task before us. But when Warwick was born in July 1973, we had no idea that the task would be rather different from the one we had so eagerly anticipated.

To begin with, all appeared normal – but he was our first child and we had no others with whom to compare him. True, he demanded a lot of attention and he cried a lot, but we assumed that all babies did this, so we had no reason to think that Warwick was any different. We didn't find it easy, however. Sometimes we were reduced to bundling him into the car and driving around to get him to sleep. And if he woke in the night, it would take us ages to quieten him down again.

'It's only wind or colic,' we were told, and then informed about the appropriate medicine. We must have fed him gallons of the stuff, but nothing helped.

At three months we took him for the usual check-up. The nurse examined him and tested his eyes to see if they were following her movements. 'He's fine,' she said. 'There's nothing wrong with him. Perhaps he's a bit slow, but he'll soon catch up.'

Joan was not so sure. In her opinion, Warwick did not seem to be following anything with his eyes. She took him to the clinic every week, but no one seemed to think there was a problem. We should have been reassured, but somehow we couldn't rest. 'If you're still worried,' said the nurse, 'have a word with the doctor.'

Within ten days of seeing the doctor, we were given an appointment to see a specialist. A few days after that,

Warwick was in hospital. The doctor had spotted petit mal, a type of epilepsy presenting frequent, mild fits. We had always thought that the small 'jumps' Warwick made were perhaps sneezes. As they hadn't happened while the nurse held him, they had gone unrecognised. We realised afterwards that the doctor had probably suspected brain damage, but Warwick remained in hospital for another six months before we were given the final diagnosis.

During this time we existed on a tide of optimism. At first we hoped the doctors would find out what was wrong with our little son. They would suggest a remedy and everything would be all right. Besides, we thought, we are Christians. God doesn't change. He healed people long ago and he can still heal now. We would pray and Warwick would be healed.

The tests continued. The doctor tested for hydro-cephalus by measuring Warwick's head, but instead of being larger, it turned out to be smaller than normal. He explained that Warwick's skull would have been normal at birth, but because it had a space inside, it had flattened during the first six months of his life. Then we were told that a biopsy would provide more information, so two little holes were bored through his skull and tiny pieces of brain tissue were removed for testing. From that they had a good idea when the damage occurred and the extent of it. It showed that around the thirtieth week of pregnancy something had caused a starvation of oxygen in the tiny baby, and this caused cerebral palsy.

The doctor prepared us for the worst. Warwick would

never lead a normal life and he might be blind and unable to walk. In his opinion, we would probably not be able to look after Warwick once he got beyond the age of about five. The only option would be full-time care. As sympathetically as possible, he advised us to go ahead and have more children and to forget about this one. Once we actually took this in, we rebelled against the idea. 'No,' we told ourselves, 'we can't do that. We will show them just what Warwick is capable of doing by making sure that every possibility of developing him is taken up.'

We understood what the doctor was trying to say. He did not mean to be cruel; he simply tried to paint the picture as black as possible so that any small step would be seen as an improvement. By this time we were under no illusions about Warwick's severe disability, but we could not agree entirely with the doctor. We had noticed that Warwick had occasional moments of recognition. Sometimes he would respond to our presence by smiling – perhaps not with definite eye contact, but we could see a reaction. This was enough to encourage us to make an effort on his behalf. We were told that Warwick's mental ability must be quite low because he didn't appear to be frustrated. We accepted that, but decided to assume that he understood everything. In this way, *we* got frustrated, but he didn't!

As the years went by we did see some improvements. To begin with, he did not go blind and he has very good hearing. He cannot speak or make any decipherable sounds, but he can make noises and he tries to join in when people around him are talking or singing. He can't walk, but moves around on his knees to where people are. He finds things to occupy himself – he plays with toys or the furniture. He can even get himself into the room he wants to be in, away from people if he prefers to be quiet. He has some independence and can make up his own mind about things in a simple way. Over a period he has developed the ability to choose from a limited selection what he wants to eat or drink. He can, to a certain extent, choose what he wears, given a choice of clothes. It is not always the best choice, however – he needs to be guided into something suitable. All his choices are 'yes' or 'no' ones. If two things are held out to him, the one to which he pays more attention is usually the one he wants.

Those who know Warwick well will recognise the occasional glint in his eye or notice the gentle smirk on his face. He may well understand far more than he is able to communicate. In addition, while some would say that he doesn't get frustrated, we think there is more going on inside than he can express. Sometimes we find sitting with him is a joy because there is a communication at some level that is different from all the normal physical ways of expression. We can sense a kind of contentment – not to mention a kind of mischief – inside him, as though he is having a game with us! As Christians with a hope of heaven, we expect that one day we will sit down and talk about these times and he'll tell us what he really heard and wanted to say.

Sometimes we can't help wondering what he would have

been like if he didn't have the disability – or what all our lives would have been like. But then, perhaps that could be thought about anyone. Maybe if they had had more education or a different personality . . . In the end, the situation must be accepted and built on as best we can, savouring the joys – for there *are* joys.

Of course, there was an element of sadness as Warwick got bigger. For the first three years before our next son, Wesley, came along, it was just like having a baby in the house – he could still be lifted and people treated him like a baby. But as he got older people didn't treat him in the same way. Some people are frightened at being confronted with disability. They see unpredictable movements and are thrown into a kind of confusion. It's a great pity, but if they don't have much contact with disabled people, they can't learn. Children are not like that. Warwick loves children – they are at his level because he is on his knees on the floor.

Both our other boys, Wesley and Matthew, got on well with Warwick. We liked them bringing their friends home to play because, to begin with, it gave these children a greater understanding of disability. They discovered that it wasn't something to be frightened of and that Warwick could play with them in his own way. We knew we'd won, however, when they came in, patted Warwick on the head and called, 'Hi, Warwick!' and got on with something else. They didn't stand and stare or try to avoid him.

At that time we were quite concerned at the way people with disabilities were viewed by the world at large and how people related to them. They seemed to be treated as less than fully human. It was around the time of the Year of the Disabled Person and the years that followed. There was an effort to get rid of the term 'handicapped' or 'mentally handicapped' and to try to use terms that were more 'politically correct' or people orientated. We tried to talk about 'people with disabilities' – they are *people* first.

We felt, therefore, that Warwick's presence in our home helped a lot of people to come to terms with people with disabilities – they *are* just people.

Recently we have consented to Warwick moving into full-time, permanent care. We knew it would have to happen one day, because our age will eventually prevent us from continuing to look after him. We felt it would be better to let him get used to a new home while we can still keep frequent contact with him. He spends weekends with us, and sometimes we like to sit with him on Sundays before he is due to return. He likes to be touched a lot and held – perhaps he needs this close contact because he can't speak – but it is at these times that we can feel a deep sadness and wonder about what might have been.

Sometimes we feel rather sorrowful – even hurt inside – because Warwick needs protecting and loving and will need this for the rest of his life. We are able to provide this only for a certain length of time. Others will have to take over from us, so we have had to come to the point where we must accept that he is now more dependent on others than on us. One day he will become totally dependent on others – he'll be on his own with whoever is caring for him.

We can't help wondering if they will care for him in the same way as we would – we who have known him all his life and understand his every movement. He will never be able to talk about his life, his hopes or aspirations like our other two sons – about how difficult or how good life is. He lives in the present and has very little past.

These are the thoughts that move me profoundly. I can do no more than hold him close. I don't want to let him go. It's a kind of grief – a bereavement – similar to when one loses a close relative. The feelings are similar. But having said that, Warwick gives something to the people around him that he could not have given if he had not been disabled. It's a sort of love different from that given by our other two boys. In a lot of ways Warwick is still a young child and loves like a young child. He has few, if any, cares. He doesn't have to worry about where his next meal is coming from or about what he has to wear. He's looked after, fed and has everything he needs. People love him because he's lovable, so he is, for the most part, happy with his lot. *We* are the ones who feel the sadness, and we have to adjust to that.

We have also had to adjust to the fact that, as Christians, we believe nothing happens by chance and that God has a plan for each of us. He allowed Warwick to be born with disabilities, but we never asked the question: 'Why has this happened to us?' One Christian acquaintance expressed the opinion that we must have done something wrong. Warwick's condition was our punishment. This unkind remark hurt us badly. We cannot believe that God punishes sin in this way.

In fact, Jesus was asked the same question by his disciples in John chapter 9: 'Rabbi, who sinned, this man or his parents, that he was born blind?' and his answer was: 'Neither this man nor his parents sinned, but this happened so that the work of God might be displayed in his life.' God has a different agenda from ours and it is one that we must accept by faith. We trust God that his work will be displayed through Warwick's life – and ours. We live in a world where lots of things are not right. Some things work properly and some don't, but somewhere in the plan of God he has seen fit to leave the world as it is – to our eyes, at least – until such time as his plan reaches fulfilment.

There is no reason to think that just because we are Christians we should be exempt from life's problems. As others suffer, so we must suffer. Christ suffered when he was here, so it should not be a surprise to us that we might suffer and that Warwick might suffer too.

Neither Joan nor I felt angry with God because he allowed our son to be born with profound disabilities. We did not fume and ask, 'Why did you let this happen?' We already knew that things go wrong for Christians as well as others. We don't live in a sort of cocoon where God 'zaps' all the wrong things, to leave us protected.

However, at that time we were living in a Christian community that believed in modern miracles. We also knew that divine intervention changed things in Bible days and occasionally it changes things nowadays. Therefore, while we accepted Warwick's disability and didn't think that it was a sign of something wrong with our relationship with God, we also believed there were times when God intervened and appeared to do amazing things. We took the example from all sorts of Bible passages where Jesus opened blind eyes, healed crippled limbs and generally restored people to some sense of full working order.

I could even quote an example from my own family. My father contracted TB meningitis in his younger days – before the advent of antibiotics. He became so ill that he was not expected to last the night. However, some of the family who were Christians, prayed for him at home at about ten o'clock that night. At exactly the same time, my father recounted, he went to sleep naturally without help, for the first time for several days. The next morning he awoke, sat up in bed and asked the nurse for breakfast. The amazed doctors did further tests and found that he was completely clear of disease. He went home a week later.

No explanation was offered other than that God had intervened, and we felt that he could still intervene for Warwick. But to believe that someone born with cerebral palsy would be healed was a tough miracle to expect! Believing that bacteria can be eradicated from the body is one thing – but to believe that actual cells could be re-formed is a miracle of biblical proportions!

I suppose we may have thought that praying for Warwick's healing would be a test of our faith. We did pray, but initially it was a 'wishful thinking' sort of prayer. Then, since we had been brought up in this community of faith, we thought we might as well go for 'the big one'.

Most Christians around us could not believe such a miracle would happen, but didn't want to hurt our feelings so went along with it. They didn't know how to tell us otherwise. Some just nodded wisely and let us carry on with our praying, while some took it up and prayed with us.

We got down to some serious prayer accompanied by one day of fasting every week. At first we prayed for the fits to stop – as a sort of sign that we were on the right track. To our joy, the fits did stop. I particularly remember the last one because it happened while we were visiting the Castle Museum in York. Then there were no more for quite some time. When Warwick came out of hospital he had been prescribed all kinds of drugs to control his fits. But these also subdued his personality. He was floppy and could not react to us because of all the sedatives he had taken. So when the fits stopped, I began to reduce his medication. Being young and foolhardy, we did not refer to medical advice, we just did it. I reduced the medicine to nothing and still the fits didn't happen. We took him to the hospital two months later and the doctor asked what medication Warwick was having.

'He isn't on anything,' I replied.

'What do you mean?' said the doctor. I explained what we believed and what had happened. 'That's amazing!' he said incredulously. 'I don't understand, but it's better for him not to be sedated. So monitor him closely and let's see how he goes on.'

From then until he was about thirteen, he didn't have another fit and neither did he have medication. We saw all kinds of little improvements that together amounted to far more than the doctors believed Warwick would ever be capable of. We thanked God for every little bit of progress. We did all we could for Warwick at the same time, of course – we took him to physiotherapy regularly and provided him with as much stimulation as possible. In addition, he went to school early because by that time our other two sons had been born and Joan had a period of ill health.

But we never saw the 'big miracle'.

We learned an enormous amount from caring for Warwick – perhaps more than we could have learned from a thousand sermons. I learned to be more patient, appreciative and caring. Perhaps if Warwick had not had the disability, we would both have been far more self-centred.

But we didn't ever get to the point where we felt a huge disappointment that Warwick had not been completely healed. We always hoped and left it all in God's hands. Eventually the hope became more rational, less 'up in the clouds'. As we got older, we understood much better how faith works. We have never stopped believing, though, and I still firmly keep the Christian hope that one day in heaven we will sit down and have a conversation with Warwick, when he will tell us what it's been like for him. We'll talk about it. But more and more now I think there won't be the big miracle that we hoped for at first. We did put a lot of effort into the prayer and fasting; although some might think it all wasted, we believe that God took all our devotion and blessed it. We continued to pray and fast until one day we realised that perhaps our efforts had become more of a ritual than anything else. The time had come to stop. We simply felt that God did not require this of us any more. Our belief in God did not change, but we began to rest in his decision rather than try to alter things.

Life settled down into a sort of pattern. We were in a caring community. There was always someone who would come around each night and pray and play with Warwick for half an hour, or maybe take him with them for an hour or so. This provided him with variety and stimulation and it also gave us a short break. Then occasionally someone would care for Warwick on a longer basis so that we could have a short holiday – we even went to Canada for a church event once.

Eventually, however, a point came in our lives when our perspective changed and our expectations and aspirations altered. We decided to leave the community and move to York, where I had a career change. I started to work in broadcasting and it brought me into contact with the world in a completely different way.

I think that even up to my mid-thirties I had lived in a slightly unrealistic world that was almost too much church and not enough world. My emergence into the world as a fully functioning human being brought me into contact with lots of ideas and so completely changed me as a person. It was almost like jumping on a helter-skelter and letting the law of gravity take over.

The world went around and around and I wondered what was happening to me. It was quite cataclysmic. Then, when the world settled down again, we held on to what we'd got – each other, Warwick, our other sons, the church. Everything had 'moved around' and changed. Now the world is rather different. We are not in that community any more and we think differently about things.

Years ago someone told us, 'Well, this is your future now,' as we looked at our helpless one-year-old firstborn in hospital. And then someone else tried to encourage us with, 'Your son is like my son.' Her son was actually about six years old and, although disabled, he was a very frustrated child and difficult to manage. I expect others would understand what she meant, but to us the picture looked very different. Our son was *not* like her son. He was not frustrated or difficult to manage, for a start. In any case, we saw him as a unique human being with his own life to live – disabled, certainly, but he couldn't be bundled together with anyone else and labelled, 'all one kind'.

Our future would be different and we would build it as we went along. We would live with whatever had to be done and God would give us grace to keep coping. In Matthew 6:34 Jesus says: 'Therefore do not worry about tomorrow, for tomorrow will worry about itself. Each day has enough trouble of its own.' God tells us not to worry about what is going to happen tomorrow, next week or next year. *Today* is what matters. God has taken care of tomorrow. We don't have to think, 'How am I going to cope for the next so-many years?' That is too over-whelming.

God hasn't given us the grace to cope with all the years to come – he has only given us the grace to live for today. Of course, there is a certain amount of planning to be done as any child gets older. But there is a sense in which you still have to take each day as it comes and ask God for the grace to cope with it.

We had to make some plans because we got to a point where we realised there would come a day when Warwick would outlive our strength and we wouldn't be physically able to provide him with a future. We had to be straight-forward with the authorities and tell them that we felt something had to be done.

We had been rather nervous about 'authorities'. We had heard horror stories about social services and the health service, but in the event we found them to be very helpful. We simply had to be honest and spell out exactly what we thought and felt. When the time came, we received a lot of support and Warwick was able to move into permanent care and live independently from us. He still needs a lot of care, but we feel more content in knowing that if anything happened to us, he would be looked after. Our local church fellowship had cared for him too, of course, and we were extremely grateful for all the loving support they gave. But it could never be more than an 'ad hoc' arrangement – for short periods, days or hours. His care now is long term – for the rest of his life.

So we are in a different phase now. For the first sixteen years of any child's life they can expect to be cared for and brought up by their parents. But Warwick is twenty-seven years old now – a man. He has his own dignity and, in a way, deserves his own independence. He doesn't want to be stuck with Mum and Dad for ever – any more than a normal 27-year-old would want to be. Parents can eventually become quite claustrophobic. Perhaps they care too much and make too many assumptions. Warwick is now more independent and can make some individual choices. He goes out shopping to buy things that we always used to buy for him. That brings a whole new dimension to his life. He has a whole new future in front of him, and that came about partly because of planning.

However, if anyone in a similar situation asked me for advice, I certainly wouldn't advise them to look ahead too far. That just isn't beneficial. Having a disabled child can be tough. You don't have the time to yourself that might be had with a child of normal abilities. By the time a normal child is twelve or thirteen years old, they are beginning to do their own thing. With a disabled child, parents don't get much time for themselves.

You are needed all the time and are very dependent on one another as a couple. We found we had to be, to make it work. We are fortunate indeed that Warwick's disability brought us together instead of dividing us, but he has put demands on our lives. We realise that life would have been quite different had he not been around. So in the end there can be fulfilment down whichever path we have to go.

I have heard it said about those with disabled children that they 'wouldn't have him or her any other way'. This is an attitude we find difficult to understand. We would have preferred that Warwick had been without the brain damage and able to achieve his full potential as a human being. He is our son, and presumably would have been similar to our other two sons – diverse, but similar. I would not wish that anyone should be disabled in any way.

Maybe people say this to affirm the disabled person. They try to ignore the fact that anything is wrong, but there *is* something wrong and it cannot be avoided. Having said that, no one is perfect – perhaps some disabilities show more than others do. Warwick's disability, however, is definable. It's a bit like being born with a limb missing or deformed. You and everyone else know that there is something wrong that could have been different. There are degrees of disability, but if it had been possible to make Warwick normal, then we would have taken that opportunity. If there had been a cure we would have looked for it. Ignoring the situation is like saying that it's no good going to the doctor when you are ill, because it's all right to be ill. We do look to improve things and we would both have loved to have seen things improve for Warwick.

And yet Warwick has somehow brought fulfilment to us and we hope we have brought it to him. There have been lots of joys along the way. Every little bit of progress is a joy in a way that wasn't the same with the other two boys. They got on in leaps and bounds and we found joy when they achieved great things. With Warwick the joys were in a smile or a look, or when he reached out for the first time, or held his own cup for the first time. Tiny things became a great joy. Daily joys. No looking ahead to the future: look for the joys *today*.

We must enjoy the here and now and leave the future to God. Take things one day at a time. Do what you have to do today and take fresh strength for tomorrow when it comes.

We may not feel very able to cope sometimes, but again God reassures us in 2 Corinthians 12:9: 'My grace is sufficient for you, for my power is made perfect in weakness.' Trusting in God is what matters. The rest is up to him.

WORDS OF HOPE AND FAITH

This short piece of Scripture sums up the changes we have been through in respect of praying for and coping with Warwick's disability. After phases of 'certainty' we arrived at a place of not knowing how to pray, only knowing that we have a certain hope and the Spirit, who prays on our behalf. What we feel is too deep for words.

Romans 8:22–7

> *We know that the whole creation has been groaning as in the pains of childbirth right up to the present time. Not only so, but we ourselves, who have the firstfruits of the Spirit, groan inwardly as we wait eagerly for our adoption as sons, the redemption of our bodies. For in this hope we were saved. But hope that is seen is no hope at all. Who hopes for what he already has? But if we hope for what we do not yet have, we wait for it patiently. In the same way, the Spirit helps us in our weakness.* **We do not know what we ought to pray for, but the Spirit himself intercedes for us with groans that words cannot express.** *And he who searches our hearts knows the mind of the Spirit, because the Spirit intercedes for the saints in accordance with God's will.*

Barrie and Joan declined to choose an additional reading for the following reason: 'We have not chosen a piece of prose or poetry. After several attempts we have agreed that in Warwick's story there are no outstanding pieces of writing that we can honestly say have helped us.'

So (writes John Young) in my capacity as Editor, I decided to choose a paragraph which I felt to be an appropriate conclusion to their chapter. It comes from the end of a famous book, published in English in 1910. The words are those of Albert Schweitzer, a brilliant scholar and controversial medical missionary.

Many Christians who have never had a dramatic spiritual experience nevertheless have a sense (perhaps fitful) of being 'accompanied' through life by the Risen Christ. Albert Schweitzer captures this experience and testifies that, very often, it is as we 'wrestle with giants' that we sense his presence most keenly.

> *He comes to us as one unknown, without a name, as of old by the lakeside. He came to those men who knew Him not. He speaks to us the same word: 'Follow thou me!' and sets us to the tasks which He has to fulfil for our time. He commands. And to those who obey Him, whether they be wise or simple, He will reveal himself in the toils, the conflicts, the suffering which they shall pass through in His fellowship, and, as an ineffable mystery, they shall learn in their own experience Who He is.*

From *The Quest of the Historical Jesus* (1906; English translation 1910)

FOR REFLECTION

1   In previous generations, severely disabled people were often kept 'out of sight'. Today, they are out and about like the rest of us. What do you think about this?

2   Barrie and Joan prayed and fasted for Warwick's wholeness. Eventually they stopped, claiming that they came to a broader understanding of what faith in God involves. Do you agree with them, or is that a rationalisation on their part? What do you make of the remarkable miracle on page 38?

3   The children who visited the Stephensons' home were initially nervous of Warwick, who seemed rather like an alien. The real breakthrough is described on page 34. What do you make of that?

4   Barrie and Joan never use the word 'handicapped', preferring to speak of 'people with disabilities'. Similarly, people who suffer from leprosy, epilepsy and cerebral palsy dislike being called lepers, epileptics and spastics. Do you share these concerns or view them as fussy 'political correctness'?

5   Stephen Hawking is one example of severe disability combined with intellectual brilliance. Despite this, the 'does he take sugar?' trap can catch us out. Do you find it easy or difficult to view people with severe disabilities as thinking, choosing, intelligent people?

3

Living with cancer:
Walter and Pauline's story

Walter and Pauline Stockdale have lived in York for most of their married life. Walter is a GP and Pauline, after teaching science for three years, left work and remained at home raising and supporting the family.

They had five children, but Andrew, their second child, died at the age of five. Their four adult children (two sons and two daughters) are all married. They have one grandchild, Joel.

They have attended St Michael-le-Belfrey Church since they arrived in York, and Walter has been a Reader for over twenty-five years (a lay preacher, for those not initiated into Anglican terminology).

'Not again, Lord! It can't be happening again!' Anger

welled up. 'But this is the third Christmas in a row that we've been confronted by cancer. *Three* Christmases that have started with "Get Well" cards! How could you allow this to strike us yet again?' The mixture of cards illogically fuelled my anger. My emotions gave vent to my feeling. I was so angry I shouted at God, the sense of let-down so intense that I could not believe it was happening. It was all so unfair!

I mentally reminded God that when Pauline's breast cancer had struck, two years before, we had accepted it as allowed by God in his perfect will. We thought it unfair, but realised that we could not expect to be any different from anyone else. Even when my cancer showed itself – suddenly and with absolutely no warning, just before Christmas once again – we wept and wondered, but had learned to trust God, the source of all healing. For two years we undertook the recommended treatment – first the surgery, followed in Pauline's case by radiotherapy and in my case by chemotherapy and immunotherapy. We struggled and wondered, but still we trusted God. Our prayers, together with those of all our wonderfully supportive friends, would bring us both through those times.

We praised and thanked our God, who commanded us in his Word, 'Be strong and courageous. Do not be afraid or terrified . . . for the LORD your God goes with you; he will never leave you nor forsake you' (Deuteronomy 31:6). We held on to those words, strong in the hope that as our healing progressed, God would be with us and lead us through.

But then, just as we began to put the experiences to the back of our minds and look to the future, Pauline discovered – just before the third Christmas – that she now had womb cancer. She was shattered to discover that she needed a hysterectomy just two years after the breast cancer. Many women have this operation, but knowing that there was a cancer there made it take on a larger significance than it perhaps should have done.

'Why, God?' I shouted silently. 'It isn't fair! Why us? Three different cancers over three successive Christmases. Where are you in all this?' There was no pretence, no denial – rather an expression of deep hurt that I could not hide. Feelings I shared later with the church as I preached on the theme of struggle.

The first nightmare began with Pauline's routine mammogram screening at a 'one-stop' clinic. When she received the recall notice, I assured her that she had no need to worry. 'They have to recall some people,' I told her confidently. 'You've no history of cancer in your family, so it'll be fine.' As a doctor of some thirty-two years, I had seen this happen several times. Only a very small percentage of mammograms indicate abnormal cells. Two weeks later, Pauline found herself in hospital for an operation to remove a lump in her breast, and I found myself eating my words.

Neither of us could believe what was happening. This kind of thing happened to others – to some of my patients, yes, but not to us. The shock coloured our thinking and affected our actions. What did the future hold? I tried not to think too far ahead.

Pauline's thoughts, however, raced ahead to the approaching Christmas and, following that, to our daughter's wedding in the spring. Her first action was to rush out to buy the ingredients to make the Christmas cake and wedding cake! Her timetable and all her carefully laid plans for the coming events were thrown into disarray. Everything must be done immediately – just in case. She dropped everything to rush to the shops and buy all outstanding Christmas presents and then set to, making the two cakes. Before long they were ready and waiting. The family would not suffer because of her disastrous news.

Pauline seemed to handle the situation rather differently from me. As soon as she heard the news she reacted practically. There were things to be done – deadlines to meet. She would never just sit down and give in to illness. As she pitched into the preparations for our daughter's wedding, her mind went into overdrive. Lots of people who had breast cancer years ago were now fine: catch the cancer early and recovery is more than likely. Removing the cancer is routine surgery nowadays. Everything will be all right – get this stage over and we can put the whole thing behind us.

After the operation, we were assured that the prognosis was good. We were urged to think positively. Pauline's attitude was that the cancer had gone and she could therefore get on with her life. She did not expect it to recur, so didn't spend time thinking about it. She considered it in the same light as, perhaps, an accident that might leave one with a bad leg. It could hurt, but the injury would not recur of itself.

A year later we were on our way back from our son's wedding in Germany when my cancer became apparent. It had been a wonderful time – a time we had been looking forward to for months. The wedding provided the back-drop to a few days' holiday in Germany and we had enjoyed every moment. On the way home, we stopped overnight in a hotel on the Dutch border.

I had no reason to think anything was wrong. There were no strange symptoms that I could recognise. But a visit to the toilet and the unexpected scarlet stream jolted me into realisation. My shocked brain could deduce only one thing: my condition was serious and bladder cancer was the likely culprit. My doctor's training, however, told me that the situation was not necessarily hopeless. Although the symptoms are startling, bladder cancer often presents early and can be halted.

The resulting examination showed that even though my cancer was aggressive, it could nevertheless be treated. Some weeks later, after intensive therapy, I was assured that for the time being the prognosis was good and the cancer had gone. Years of checks at four-monthly intervals would follow, but I could thank God for healing now.

Then, with deadly accuracy, as another Christmas approached, we were horrified to discover that Pauline now had womb cancer.

'I felt that I had been knocked down yet again. This was our third occurrence of cancer and I seemed to find it harder to get up on to my feet this time,' Pauline told me. 'The hardest thing at the time was not being able to lift our little grandson or play with him as I would normally have done. I felt a little excluded from life – pushed out to the fringes. I was aware of feeling very low during the grey days of January and I found it hard to find the energy to get going again. I realised that I needed the company of other people and made use of friends to get myself out of the house. Then gradually my spirits lifted. My task over the Christmas holiday was to write an essay with the title, "An autobiography of my spiritual journey". Once I got into it, and started to look back over my life, I saw how faithful God had been to me. That was a wonderful tonic.'

We were, however, relieved when we found out that it wasn't a secondary cancer but a result of the drugs used to combat the breast cancer. We were assured that its removal would probably be the end of it. 'Again we thank you,' I told God, 'but was it really necessary to take us through three Christmases of uncertainty and trauma?'

'I can hardly believe this has happened to us three times,' said Pauline. 'I would have thought that if one of us contracted cancer, then the chances of the other one getting it would have been remote. The statistics are surely heavily against such a thing happening to both husband and wife.'

'Statistics can say what they like,' I argued, 'but when it happens to you, you are one hundred per cent involved. Statistics don't promise anything. They just talk about possibilities.'

As my anger subsided, so did my questions. We may have been Christians for a long time, but God still had many things to teach us. Perhaps that was the right way to approach the problem, but at the time it was all happening I felt confused and unable to understand. It's only looking back that some things have become clearer.

The initial surgery removed glands from under Pauline's arm. She had been afraid that she wouldn't be able to use her arm properly again, but her fears were unfounded. She looked quite normal and could do more or less all she could do before, but since the operation she has suffered quite a lot of aching. She seemed to rebel against this in a way.

'It's an illogical feeling, really,' she told me. 'I feel as though I've been attacked. My arm was invaded by surgery – unexpected surgery – and I feel violated to some extent. I know this is silly and that the operation prevented the spread of the cancer, but I can't help feeling a bit annoyed – I can't think why!'

I, on the other hand, had a slightly different experience. My bladder cancer having been removed, I could rest assured – but only until the next health check in four months' time. My life is just as full and active as it has always been, but now I live in the light of the next health check. I am well – for the time being. The checks are not very pleasant, either, so I don't look forward to them very much. I cannot, therefore, forget the cancer and live oblivious to it. I am always aware of the next check until Graeme, my surgical friend, looks down the scope at the bladder wall and says, 'That looks fine, Walter. Do you want to have a look?' Then I can rest until next time.

Of course, I don't expect to hear him say, 'Oh, I'm sorry . . .' I don't live in fear of a recurrence, but it would be a devastating blow if ever that happened.

Pauline found it harder to cope when I was diagnosed as having bladder cancer than she did at having cancer herself. I suspect that having me under her feet for two months contributed to that! She had to cope with my illness and she had to watch me coping with it, too. The two did not always coincide! She didn't always have the opportunity to talk with friends without me hearing all that was said. So she suppressed her own feelings, and that proved isolating at times.

Sometimes we imagine that as Christians we should all respond in the same way. Why we should think like that when we are all unique, I'm not quite sure. But we found it hard to talk about these differences when we were both feeling anxious. When I was poorly she would put me first, and perhaps that's why she found the job of carer the harder task.

We did both feel stilled and more peaceful when we could stay in the present moment. These times of anxiety, however, did remind us of the things that really matter to us – our relationships with each other, our family and our friends and, not least, our relationship with God.

Pauline found it helpful to have a 'safe place' – a happy, familiar place to be, where, in her imagination, she could sit and be with Jesus. Then, when she felt she didn't know how to pray, or couldn't pray – or even when she felt down or scared – she could go to her 'safe place' and, without words, be with Jesus. She found that she got frightened when things didn't go as she had expected. It was helpful having people who had been through it before and were now fine, but everybody's experience is slightly different.

At first Pauline was absolutely sure that the breast cancer would never return. It took time to accept the reality of the possibility of that happening. She felt that it was like making a journey – things change along the way. New things come into view as the journey goes on. The most helpful thing was that, in all the changes, God remained the same. The image of God being a rock or an anchor became more real for her, even at those times when she felt angry or frustrated about life not being fair!

Another helpful thing was having a goal to aim for after the operation and radiotherapy. Following our daughter's wedding, Pauline had arranged for a group of us to walk the West Highland Way. This is a one-hundred-mile trek from Glasgow to Fort William. This we did over the Spring Bank Holiday week. The completion of the walk was surrounded with a great feeling of exhilaration and celebration, with Pauline being the focus.

During my illness I moved from a place of 'waiting to get better' to a place of accepting that I had to live with this illness – at least for the time being. Then, suddenly, the illness was not dominating our lives and everything became more normal again. No one knows what is around the next corner as far as the future is concerned. The difference is that now we are aware of 'not knowing', whereas before we had these cancers we never thought about our plans ever being interrupted!

Throughout our three years of uncertainty we were grateful to have the care and support of many friends and acquaintances. In fact, we found that we didn't need the excellent after-care support of the cancer care nurses. It was very reassuring to know that they were there to answer any questions we might have, no matter how insignificant we thought these might be. We were assured that we could telephone at any time and always find someone willing to talk us through any problem, however small. We were never to feel that we were 'bothering' anyone. But, in the event, we had so much support from those around us that official support services were not needed at all. In fact, we had to admit that sometimes the thoughtfulness of our friends became – just a little – overwhelming!

To begin with I had my colleagues in the practice to turn to. I could discuss the medical details with them, should I need to, but Pauline and I both had many friends within and without the church who showed us overwhelming love and care. From the start, we received a staggering outpouring of concern – lots of cards and very practical love. It was wonderful to experience, but sometimes difficult to handle!

Our phone became an object of doubtful pleasure. When at home, we found ourselves constantly at the mercy of its insistent ringing. If we went out we would return to a tape full of concerned enquiries, which would take us for ever to respond to! Such well-meaning people – all praying for us, supporting us and enquiring after us.

Part of the problem came about because of my public standing in the community. I've been around for a long time and have always tried to be open with people. I've encouraged my patients to be open with me about their problems, and have been free to be open with them about myself. It follows, therefore, that people feel no compunction about contacting me and discussing their problems, and in the same forthright way they showed their concern for Pauline and myself.

I was particularly touched by the remarks of one of my patients as he left my surgery. In response to his request about my health, I had mentioned that I would be having another check-up the following week. 'I'll pray for you next week,' he said. *He* was caring for *me* – our roles were reversed! The amazing thing was that I didn't really know that this man was a Christian at all.

And this kind of thing happened quite often. So many of my patients showed a watchful interest in my progress. They asked how I felt and when my next check-up would be. It was interesting and, I thought, rather unusual. The relationship between doctor and patient changed. The general idea is that the doctor does the caring. You visit his surgery to be looked after and sorted out, and the needs of the doctor are rarely considered. But in my case a sort of 'chemistry' happened, whereby mutual caring took place. I had shared the problems of many of my patients over the years. Now they were sharing mine. This was very special.

It was wonderful to experience such thoughtfulness, but at home it became rather a practical problem. In retrospect, what we needed was a willing person to become the focus of the enquiries for us. Someone who would take on the task of providing news bulletins to anyone who called so that we could forget the phone and concentrate our minds on getting well. Someone who could fend off yet again the 'old chestnut': 'Surely not – doctors don't get ill!'

However, perhaps the fact that this doctor got ill has shown a positive aspect to others suffering in a similar way. My openness has helped to diffuse the fear in people's minds. It *is* possible to overcome the demon called cancer.

But in the same way that I am open with my illness, I am also open with my Christianity. I could not make a secret of my anger at God for allowing all this to happen, but at the same time I did not lose my faith. I didn't say, 'There can't be a God if he lets this happen,' or consider all my years of Christian witness to be worth nothing, simply because God didn't protect us from illness. Perhaps in my early years as a Christian my attitude might have been different. Those young in the faith do sometimes tend to think that becoming a Christian will protect them from adversity. But God doesn't work that way.

God doesn't pick out Christians to bless and leave the others. That isn't what Christianity is about. The amazing fact about being a Christian is that through the death and resurrection of Jesus, we have a relationship with God, our Heavenly Father. Whatever the circumstances of our life or death, nothing can separate us from the love that God has for us. What we have to learn is that Christ is *with us* in the suffering. God is always the same. We move or get knocked over or buffeted about, but God doesn't change at all. That knowledge is a great anchor. God is the Rock (Romans 8:38–9).

All this seemed important to us while we were being shaken by illness. It seemed as though the earth was being knocked from under us, but God was actually the same. He has not changed simply because we are ill. His relationship with us does not change – from his point of view. *We* are the ones who change. It is *our* attitude to *him* that suffers, if we allow it to do so. I knew all this. I had known it for many years, but after the third cancer reared its ugly head I must admit that I allowed myself to question God – to 'have a go' at him!

'Come on, Lord,' I railed, 'this just isn't fair! Once, yes. Twice, even – but *three* times?' My many years of fellowship with God taught me that he would never turn his back on me simply because I became angry. God understands our frailty, our emotions and our reactions and he is great enough to absorb our anger. I can be 'real' with God! The result has been that my faith has become deeper and I have become more aware of my own feelings. Having been a very 'out there' sort of person in the past – an extravert many times over – I have been forced to a greater awareness of my emotions and myself. I now understand that it is all right to express one's true feelings to God.

There is no reason to feel guilty. Before our illnesses I might have felt that to express anger to God would be a denial of my faith. But there has been quite a perceptible move in me towards the acceptance of my feelings. They are a valid part of my experience. God accepts me *with* my anger rather than condemning me for it. To understand that his love is there for me in that anger, as well as in every other aspect of my suffering, has given me a new view of myself and a better understanding of God.

Why I should have been so angry with God is another question. It wasn't because I thought we were going to die. I have no illusions about my own mortality. We all have to die sooner or later, and Pauline and I are not young people any more! As a doctor I understand only too well that all sorts of other things, like heart attacks or whatever, are more likely to happen before cancer catches up with me. No, anticipation of death did not cause my anger. As Christians, Pauline and I, while acknowledging the unknown, have a confidence about life after death.

However, there is an understandable fear of the *process* of dying – the possible pain, loss of control and identity. We belong to the Lord Jesus Christ, who has promised eternal life with him to all who believe (John 3:16). Death, for us, therefore, will be both the continuation and the beginning of eternity with our Heavenly Father. I think the perspectives of my values were challenged – as, I'm sure, are everyone's when faced with serious illness.

Threatening illnesses such as cancer can cause their victims to react in one of two ways. Either they anticipate death and fear it, or they think positively in terms of values and quality of life.

Pauline and I both accept that our cancers are under control and we expect to remain free of them. But we are not young any more. We have had to accept that we have a limited time in front of us. Having cancer, however, has perhaps heightened our awareness of our mortality. It has made us take stock of our lives as never before. We have already had to come to terms with my approaching retirement, with its inference of diminishing years ahead. We both now agree that relationships and values are more important to us than anything. Suddenly we have both realised that the greater parts of our lives are behind us, and that we must make the most of the future. Suddenly our relationship with each other has taken on a greater significance, for we have come to realise that the cancers *could* have curtailed that remaining time.

Throughout our lives, all sorts of aims and objectives have clouded our thinking – some rightly, some wrongly. But then, as now, relationships and values probably ought to have taken a higher profile. Perhaps it is only at our time of life that we come to understand how important our relationships are – husband and wife, parents and children, friends and relations, but most importantly our relationship with God. These are the objectives we are now looking to address most particularly, and this, I think, is what God is trying to say to us today.

God allowed me my anger. Some of my patients who find themselves stricken with cancer have a different reaction. They feel guilty or even dirty. There are even those who think – albeit sometimes subconsciously – that the cancer is some kind of a 'marker', indicating something evil about them. Perhaps it is a judgement on their past life? Some people almost want to identify with that and struggle with the sense of guilt caused by the illness and with the sin in their lives. People often use emotive language when they talk about cancer.

My concern is never to deny the truth of illness, but to put alongside that truth other very special truths about those who think this way – their infinite value as a person whatever the unpleasant realities are. They are very special people – unique and precious to God, no matter what their background. I try to explore this aspect with them, rather than letting them become pre-occupied with illness, be it cancer or whatever. I aim to point out the wholeness of truth about them so that they have some hope for the future, rather than seeing it simply in terms of death. In other words, it's not just talking about death, but about heaven. There are two sides to the dying process.

We have shared our story, but at this present time we are well. We are aware that many others are facing more worrying circumstances. Some face progressive illness, others face clinically hopeless situations and terminal disease. We don't know what it is like to be in that situation. What we have shared has been much more about living with cancer and going through the experience of having had cancer, but it is certainly not about dying from cancer.

We had one dear woman at church who was very frightened to be honest about her condition, because she thought that all Christians should be very pleased that they were dying and going to be with Jesus. This unreal attitude somehow prevented her from saying how she felt and how frightened she was about dying. I found that very sad. Christians are only human. God has instilled within us a love of life; faced with death it is natural to be frightened. There is no guilt in that. At the same time I would encourage people to be honest and to find somebody who will listen to them, encourage them and allow them to explore their feelings.

It is rather easier for the Christian because of the hope of heaven, but non-Christians may also want to explore their feelings and to learn more of this Christian hope of heaven.

The Good News of Jesus Christ is that 'God so loved the world that he gave his one and only Son, that whoever believes in him shall not perish but have eternal life' (John 3:16). This hope comes out of God's tremendous love for each individual.

This is a situation where the Christian has a very real message of hope for the unbeliever, and the hope comes out of their value as seen by God – his particular love for them. Their illness, whatever it is, is not about alienating them from God and his love. It is about directing their thoughts and hopes towards him – and this is the direction that Pauline and I will be taking in the years remaining to us.

WORDS OF HOPE AND FAITH

Pauline: It was this love of God, in the midst of the storm going on around us, that was an anchor for me. Somehow, probably through everyone's prayers for me, I could really hold on to that.

Romans 8:38–9

> *For I am convinced that neither death nor life, neither angels nor demons, neither the present nor the future, nor any powers, neither height nor depth, nor anything else in all creation, will be able to separate us from the love of God that is in Christ Jesus our Lord.*

I have also found the following in some notes I wrote at the time:

> *I knew I had to let God in at a deeper level of myself. I read Matthew 16:21, 24 in the paraphrase version* The Message *by Eugene Peterson. It reads, 'Anyone who intends to come with me has to let me lead. You're not in the driver's seat; I am. Don't run from suffering; embrace it. Follow me and I'll show you how . . .'*

Walter: Psalm 40, with other psalms such as 27, 34 and 139, reveals a person who is honest with God, both in pain and in joy, without fear of retribution. This was and is an encouragement to be real with God and to look for him in the dark places. Such an approach helps to maintain hope and faith in God who is always present with and for me.

Psalm 40

I waited patiently for the LORD;
   he turned to me and heard my cry.
He lifted me out of the slimy pit,
   out of the mud and mire;
he set my feet on a rock
   and gave me a firm place to stand.
He put a new song in my mouth,
   a hymn of praise to our God.
Many will see and fear
   and put their trust in the LORD.

Blessed is the man
   who makes the LORD his trust,
who does not look to the proud,
   to those who turn aside to false gods.
Many, O LORD my God,
   are the wonders you have done.
The things you planned for us
   no-one can recount to you;
were I to speak and tell of them,
   they would be too many to declare.

Sacrifice and offering you did not desire,
   but my ears you have pierced;
burnt offerings and sin offerings
   you did not require.

Then I said, 'Here I am, I have come —
  it is written about me in the scroll.
I desire to do your will, O my God;
  your law is within my heart.'

I proclaim righteousness in the great assembly;
  I do not seal my lips, as you know, O LORD.
I do not hide your righteousness in my heart;
  I speak of your faithfulness and salvation.
I do not conceal your love and your truth
  from the great assembly.

Do not withhold your mercy from me, O LORD;
  may your love and your truth always protect me.
For troubles without number surround me;
  my sins have overtaken me, and I cannot see.
They are more than the hairs of my head,
  and my heart fails within me.

Be pleased, O LORD, to save me;
  O LORD, come quickly to help me.
May all who seek to take my life
  be put to shame and confusion;
may all who desire my ruin
  be turned back in disgrace.
May those who say to me, 'Aha! Aha!'
  be appalled at their own shame.
But may all who seek you
  rejoice and be glad in you;

may those who love your salvation
always say,
'The LORD be exalted!'

Yet I am poor and needy;
may the Lord think of me.
You are my help and my deliverer;
O my God, do not delay.

Pauline chose the following poem by John Newton because it forms a 'commentary' on those words from Matthew 16.

Be still, my heart! These anxious cares
To thee are burdens, thorns and snares,
They cast dishonour on the Lord
And contradict His gracious word.

Brought safely by His hand thus far,
Why wilt thou now give place to fear?
How canst thou want if He provide?
Or lose thy way with such a guide?

When first, before His mercy-seat,
Thou didst to Him thy all commit,
He gave thee warrant from that hour
To trust His wisdom, love and power.

Did ever trouble yet befall
And He refuse to hear thy call?

71

And has He not His promise passed,
That thou shalt overcome at last?

He who has helped me hitherto
Will help me all my journey through,
And give me daily cause to raise
New Ebenezers to His praise.

Though rough and thorny be the road,
It leads thee home apace to God;
Then count thy present trials small,
For heaven will make amends for all.

John Newton, 1725–1807

FOR REFLECTION . . .

1   Max Wigley and Barrie and Joan Stephenson seem not to have experienced anger. Walter Stockdale did. Does that mean that Max, Barrie and Joan have a stronger faith than Walter? Or is it a question of different personalities and circumstances?

2   Three cancers in three Christmases for committed Christians. Why didn't God protect them? Walter and Pauline don't talk explicitly about praying for healing (although they do say that they were upheld by the love and prayers of many friends). Does that surprise you?

3   How open and honest should we be about the giants

with whom we wrestle? We all need a few people with whom we can share our problems, fears and hopes. But is it wise to 'wear our hearts on our sleeves' for all to see? Or is this entirely a matter of personality and circumstance?

4   Belief in heaven and eternal life is an enormous comfort when confronting death. But it can be misapplied, as it was by the woman on page 67. Do you know people for whom Christian belief in heaven is a strength – or a snare (leading to denial of our true feelings)? What about you?

5   Each contributor was invited to select a Bible passage and a poem or piece of prose which they found helpful. What would you have chosen?

4

Living with bereavement: Chris's story

Chris discovered the joys of education as an adult, having failed her eleven-plus exam. Following her degree course at York University she studied for an Advanced Diploma and Master's Degree in Counselling. Chris has her own counselling practice and is Staff Counsellor for St Leonard's Hospice in York. She also leads training courses and teaches in a local prison. Chris is a member of St Paul's Church in York. She has two adult children and two adorable cats.

When Joyce, in her sixties, came to me for counselling, she had reached crisis point. Her husband had died some years before, but with the loving support of her children and her church she had coped, she thought, reasonably well. Eventually an opportunity arose to move house, and then, to her bewilderment, she found herself beset with strange fears. The fears increased until panic and fright left her feeling unable to venture even outside her front door. In desperation she came to see me. As we talked it became clear that she was bewildered and frightened but did not relate her feelings in any way to her husband's death.

'I got through John's death without falling to pieces – why should this happen now, just when my life seems to be coming together?' she asked me.

From my work as a counsellor I was aware that stress related to the loss of a loved one can surface in many guises. I asked Joyce about the circumstances of her husband's death.

It transpired that their marriage had been happy but problematic. Her husband had suffered a prolonged and very difficult illness before he died, during which Joyce had cared for him bravely. It had been hard for her to come to terms with the disaster which was engulfing them both. She confessed to me that she had felt anger and bitterness that their marriage should end in that way. In addition, as a Christian, she felt obliged to 'put a brave face' on her suffering and suppress her feelings.

Joyce tormented herself with guilt and tried to hide the unwelcome feelings of betrayal and anger at her plight. Then, after John died, she felt obliged to suppress her grief. After all, she knew that he had gone to be with the Lord and was therefore at peace and happy in God's presence. Deep down, however, *she* did not feel much peace in this knowledge. She felt – illogically, she knew – angry that John had left her. She felt bitter that she had been left to pick up the pieces of life and carry on, and guilty that she should have such feelings. Joyce also struggled to suppress relief that the task of nursing him – which had drained her physically and emotionally – was now over. Waves of guilt and shame swept over her and she fought to subdue them. She had loved her husband deeply, but problems in their marriage had caused wounds she tried hard to forget. Such confused feelings caused further anguish, so she buried them deep within herself.

I began to explain gently that these feelings are quite normal. Joyce did not have to fight her feelings. She could express them and work through them. In fact, after a bereavement, anger is not necessarily aimed in one direction. It can be focused anywhere. It can be deflected to someone or something other than the loved one. Some bereaved people will focus their anger on God or the medical profession, or even themselves. However, anger directed towards the loved one is particularly difficult to cope with or justify to oneself.

Joyce's anger had turned into anxiety and fear. She became unsure of herself, and nervous. Her unconscious fear of losing control became focused on her surroundings. She wanted to control everything in order to be safe. This eventually revealed itself in a fear of going beyond her front door. Moving outside began to trigger panic attacks, until eventually she became too fearful to venture out and found herself trapped indoors. A paradox had been created: 'I want to go out but if I do I will panic, so I will stay in.' Then, 'If I always stay in, I feel trapped.' This caused a 'no win' situation of anxiety which brought her into counselling. She needed to take the risk of identifying her sense of betrayal and her powerlessness, and bring these into the open. Then she would begin to feel more in control.

As she began to work with her feelings in therapy, she became less subject to anxiety and panic. She allowed herself to go back and move through the grieving process, letting out the feelings that had become trapped and which, in turn, had become a trap for her.

If I could have talked with Joyce before her husband died, there are a number of suggestions I would have made. Joyce had the chance to prepare for the inevitable bereavement. In the case of sudden death, of course, no emotional preparation is possible. But when the illness is protracted, as it was for Joyce's husband, a multitude of emotions and feelings will be experienced.

The best preparation is to try to say everything you've always wanted to say to the person who is ill. Take the opportunity to express things you may have held back before – love, gratitude, memories, apologies. One of the most difficult problems suffered by the bereaved is a sense of regret that one cannot make up for lost time. They so often wish they could go back and say all those things that were left unsaid. Talking won't prevent the grief or pain of the eventual loss, but it will help to know that everything you want or need to say has been said.

Times of approaching loss are also times when families

can take the opportunity to make amends for past hurts – to face some of the things that have to be faced; to repair rifts and find a way, through sharing, to forgiveness. However, not all people have loving or appreciative thoughts that they would like to express to the dying. Some struggle with negative feelings. What ought to be done in such a situation? The outcome could mean long-lasting guilt either way for the one still living. There are no easy answers.

Personally, I would ask the person to look inside. Would what they would like to say be 'heard' by the one who is dying? Would the results of 'unburdening' be helpful and healing?

There are ways of approaching negative things that have to be said and there are gentle ways of doing such things. Elisabeth Kübler-Ross, who writes a lot about death and bereavement, believes in honesty. She believes that if both parties can be honest with each other, healing can take place. I think one just has to be sensitive about what really needs to be said – what would be helpful to the one dying and what would be helpful for the one left.

One of the highlights for me over the last few years was meeting Dame Cicely Saunders, founder of the Hospice Movement. In a recent newspaper interview she spoke movingly about the death of her own husband. She and her husband had said all they wanted to say and she has no regrets about words unspoken. 'The way people die has a big effect on the way their families live on afterwards,' she says. 'If you have a complicated relationship with someone before they die, it can be very difficult afterwards.

Sometimes it's hard to forgive, but forgiveness is releasing. Often they leave a strengthened family, despite the loss' (*Daily Mail*, 26 February 2000).

Bereavement, however, is not simply confined to the loss of a close human being. So often this is the association made, but people go through all kinds of loss: losing one's job, losing a pet, children leaving home, going through certain transitional periods in life – like the menopause (male or female!). All these are losses which can actually bring the same sort of feelings as that of the bereavement of a loved one, including shock, anger, anxiety and loneliness. In fact, sometimes they carry an added burden because this kind of loss is not recognised as bereavement by the people around, or even by the bereaved themselves, and so it is not mourned. Further, the bereaved will not talk about it in the way he or she might if the loss concerned a person.

Society is increasingly recognising that miscarriage also comes into this category. The expectant parents have lost a child – no matter that it had not grown to full term. Abortion, too, can bring unexpected and complicated grief reactions which are particularly hard to deal with.

Childlessness and disability also mean a loss of hopes and dreams. For many the prospect of healthy children is an important part of what they expect life to hold. Childlessness can result in a series of mini bereavements as expectation and loss follow month by month.

If someone has experienced several bereavements over a period of time, the experience can become increasingly difficult. We don't 'get used' to bereavement so that the pain is less. Each loss carries its own pain. Multiple losses will almost certainly make life even more difficult.

However well prepared we think we are, loss always comes as a shock. We might liken it to childbirth: parents go to all the ante-natal classes and find out exactly what is going to happen, but still, when birth actually occurs, the effect is overwhelming.

However, current research shows that good preparation, if this is possible, can make bereavement easier to bear. Each loss is a personal tragedy that must be lived through – and it *can* be lived through. It is not a tragedy that has to end in failure. It can become the door into a new life – a different way of living, the start of something new.

There is a pattern to coping with bereavement – although it is also a very individual process depending on the relationships of those involved and, indeed, one's relationship to God. For instance, coping with the death of a child is very different from that of coping with the death of an elderly parent. There is a sense of inevitability and right order about losing our parents, whereas we feel a sense of injustice and outrage about the loss of a child.

My own experience of bereavement was to do with the loss of my marriage. After twenty-five years my marriage irretrievably broke down and we separated. Struggling with my husband to find a way to stay married was not a new thing for us, so, when finally we decided to part, I expected to find relief rather than grief.

In fact the experience of loss was so unexpected and powerful that I felt utterly bereft, as though I hardly knew who I was. I felt that everywhere I went I was looking for something, for someone, who would make sense of my life. The powerful unconscious forces of this loss reaction are described in the following extract of the grief-like behaviour of the Greylag goose experiencing the loss of its life-long mate.

> The first response of the disappearance of the partner consists in the anxious attempt to find him again. The goose moves about restlessly by day and night, flying great distances and visiting places where the partner might be found, uttering all the time the penetrating trisyllabic long distance call. The searching expeditions are extended farther and farther and quite often the searcher itself gets lost, or succumbs to an accident.
>
> All the objective observable characteristics of the goose's behaviour on losing its mate are roughly identical with human grief.

Lorenz, quoted in *Grief Counselling and Grief Therapy* by J. William Worden (1991)

This sort of grief is triggered when we lose those things that make up our sense of self and those people and intimacies that give structure and meaning to our life. The Greylag goose was searching, literally, for his other half. He had lost sight of who he was without his mate. Human beings experience the same reactions to loss and we need to go through a pattern of grief which helps us to reorientate ourselves to a very different life – a life without our loved one. This, of course, takes time.

Colin Murray Parkes is a psychologist who has made a special study of loss. He identifies four stages in the process of grief. As I look back on my own grief process I find it is hard to separate out the various stages of bereavement which he describes, but I can identify with many of the related feelings and physical sensations which each stage brings. It must be remembered, however, that these four stages are only rough guides to a complex process.

First, there is a feeling of numbness when the bereaved seems to feel nothing. Shock and disbelief seem to suspend reality. This moves into a yearning and a searching – as we saw with the Greylag goose. During this stage it is not unknown for people to hallucinate, maybe seeing their loved one walking down the street, in the supermarket or across the road. Eventually the full realisation of our loss hits hard. We protest that life is not fair. Just when we are lacking in motivation or energy, we find that a whole new set of skills must be learned in order to live a new kind of life. Then we are beset by loneliness and bewilderment.

The third phase of our mourning brings disorganisation and despair. Questions like 'How can I ever get my life together?' and 'How can I cope?' press in. This may be accompanied by a descent into depression, with feelings of hopelessness, helplessness and fear. This stage can be made more difficult if it happens some considerable time after the bereavement, when friends and relations are expecting the bereaved person to be 'getting over' the loss.

Often there can be a lot of guilt because of the unspoken expectation of those around, who are desperately hoping to see an improvement in spirits. Consequently the bereaved may feel obliged to stop talking about the loss and try to hide their feelings. But suppressing your feelings will not help the bereavement process. The best thing to do in these circumstances is to find a good and trusted friend or counsellor to whom you can talk about your loss. Such feelings do not mean that you are failing. It is simply another part of the process.

By the time Joyce came to me for help, she had suppressed many of her feelings. She thought she was coping well because she hid them. It was not until they surfaced as chronic anxiety and panic about going out that she knew she needed to talk. If she had found a friend at the time of her husband's death who allowed her to pour out her anger and bitterness as well as her sadness and loss, she might have avoided the later crisis.

Joyce had got stuck in the grieving process. Important issues had not been identified or worked through. I have known people who have become locked into the first stage of denial for years because the fact of the loss was simply not accepted.

This may well happen at the death of a child – one of the most difficult bereavements. Refusal to recognise the loss can lead to deep unconscious denial: the bereaved wants everything to remain the same – the child's room, for instance, must be left exactly as it was. The child cannot be 'released' because the pain of separation feels too overwhelming to allow any changes.

This kind of reaction can happen with other bereavements, too. Clues that might identify such a reaction can be a recurring pattern of actions or situations with which the bereaved person cannot cope. They may see something on television, for instance, which will trigger a sense of panic and fear.

Joyce's problem was triggered by her change of house to a new, less familiar place. The suppressed grief surfaced. Her son recognised a problem and persuaded Joyce to seek help.

Over the next few weeks Joyce began to recognise her grief and talk through her real feelings, and started to release the deep pain and fear she had unwittingly held back. This enabled her to move into the final stage of grief and mourning – that of acceptance.

Acceptance was difficult for Joyce, but for some people it can come very quickly after their bereavement: for example, those who care for Alzheimer sufferers or who carry the burden of caring through terminal illness. It is possible for them to experience their grief and mourning before the actual point of death. They experience the loss of their loved one as they watch them change over a period of time into someone different – so unlike the person they knew. When death itself comes there may be none of the shock or anger or helplessness that often comes at the point of death, just a true sense of sadness and relief. Finally, as Jesus himself said, 'It is finished.'

Human beings are wonderful creatures. We find ways

of surviving. But surviving is not the same as living. A new way of being *can* be discovered. It will be different from the life led before the death of the loved one, but it will be possible to live life satisfactorily once more. Joyce eventually found a way of living without her husband, painful though the process initially proved to be.

Colin Murray Parkes calls this final stage, 'reorganisation'. It brings relief to the bereaved because a point of acceptance has been reached. Sometimes 'acceptance' is a difficult word for those suffering loss. It smacks of 'forgetting' or 'ignoring', but this is far from the truth. It certainly doesn't mean that tears won't be shed any more or that the pain has disappeared for ever.

It does mean, however, that the bereaved has found a way to work through grief so that life can go on – complete with precious memories. The sense of the presence of the lost person can be retained in the heart. Anniversaries can be remembered. Fun and laughter can be recalled. Tears shed are tears of poignancy, not pain. When this happens, the grief becomes manageable and not an overwhelming pit of suffering.

When Paul McCartney's wife, Linda, died of cancer in 1998, everyone could feel his grief and sense of loss. In an interview Paul explained how he had talked and cried endlessly with his children and his friends as he worked through his grief. He did not hide the pain, but released it through sharing with others who listened willingly.

There could be no doubt about the couple's close relationship. So when the interviewer asked whether he might ever think of entering into another relationship, we might have thought the prospect would be impossible for him. He had lost a loving soul-mate with whom he had shared many years of happiness. How could he possibly ever replace her? But Paul had grieved effectively. He had not hidden his feelings but released them in a healing flow. He had now reached the point where he could actually imagine someone else in his life. The memories of Linda and the wonderful life they shared would never be erased and never replaced, but another partner would bring a new lease of life – different from the last, but just as fulfilling.

The loss of a loved one can never be erased, of course. Anniversaries come around regularly and all the memories are revived anew. The first year is particularly acute as every memory is continually recalled. However, for some the second year is even worse. Friends think that the grieving is past and the worst is over. Even the bereaved may expect this, and it comes as something of a shock to discover that the pain is still there. We may shed painful tears alone, struggling with the pain in solitude.

But crying is good. It is important to realise that our loss will never be forgotten – nor should it be. The pain will recur at times throughout life. This is normal and right. I remember my own dear grandmother shedding tears for the loss of her baby who had died fifty years before. This had nothing to do with a difficult or abnormal bereavement. It was just that something had triggered a memory of her much loved baby daughter. She felt the pain once again, and, like Jesus, she wept.

There is an added dimension when the bereaved is a Christian. Death to the Christian refers to the body only. The soul – the real personality – lives on, and to a believer, that means being at one with Christ in heaven. We have Jesus' promise of everlasting life. This *can* put the bereaved under additional pressure to be glad that the loved one is in heaven, restored and happy. We know that the comfort of God is assured at such a time of loss. This might lead to guilty feelings about having negative emotions. Grief can then seem to be a failure of faith and something to be resisted.

There is a wonderfully reassuring passage in the book of Acts. Stephen, the first Christian martyr, had suffered a terrible death by stoning. As he died he was given a glimpse of heaven. The gates of glory were flung open and he saw Jesus standing to receive him.

But, despite this, we do not read that his fellow believers rejoiced with him. On the contrary, we are told that 'godly men buried Stephen and mourned deeply for him' (Acts 8:2). Their friend had died and they wept – for themselves.

The fact is that Christians cannot regard their faith as some form of 'insurance policy' against suffering. We cannot expect to avoid grief and hurt simply because we have faith in God. We are human beings whose emotions are affected by death – or, indeed, by any other trauma. So we must expect to go through the normal processes triggered by such a devastating event. Trying to avoid the natural process of grief is likely to cause trouble and will make moving on impossible.

Fiona Castle, who so publicly faced the terminal cancer and ultimate death of her husband Roy, reflects on her experience: 'There were still days when I thought my heart would break and that I would explode with the grief and helplessness of it all, but on the whole the time passed quickly as I coped with daily duties and needs as they arose. It is as if the human heart can only bear so much agony and hurt, and we take refuge in normal life' (*Give Us This Day*, Kingsway Publications, 1993).

Having said that, Christians often say that they *do* feel inexplicably comforted in their loss. They may feel a sense of the Lord's presence and a reassurance that their loved one is safe in heaven. Faith, then, can certainly help in various ways.

Christians may find their faith rocked and tested. However, the Lord is very gracious, and when everything else is stripped away, the true kernel of faith often becomes a reality. God never leaves his children to suffer alone.

He has promised to comfort us in our sufferings. Just before his ascension Jesus said, 'I am with you always, to the very end of the age.' He will never break that promise. He understands our doubts and fears as we face our losses. Be honest with God and allow yourself to tell him all your feelings. Read the psalms and ponder the fact that the psalmist poured everything into his prayers. Joy and praise, yes, but anger and bewilderment too.

I believe that death, whether one is a Christian or not, is sacred ground, and when we approach it we enter a huge mystery. We are touched by this mystery as we enter into the pain of loss. It becomes part of our lives as we journey on and through into a new life. Part of this mystery is seen in the transformation of lives. For many, loss and pain becomes a wellspring of creativity and life. Leah Betts' father has campaigned ceaselessly for drugs awareness, following the death of his daughter through Ecstasy tablets. Tim Parry's parents have been instrumental in the opening of a Peace Centre for young people, following the death of their son in the IRA bombing in Warrington. Gordon Wilson became a symbol for peace and reconciliation in Northern Ireland, following the death of his daughter Marie in the bombing at the Remembrance Day Service in Enniskillen. The mystery of life and death touches us all.

Finally, Fiona Castle, who has just celebrated the completion of the Roy Castle Centre for Cancer Research, speaks very movingly about this mystery as she sees it:

I know that death is something to be faced, but not feared. It is the ultimate statistic – one hundred per cent of all people die . . . Yet many people spend their entire lives hiding from the very thought of it, and allow their fear of what may happen to them or their loved ones to colour their whole lives. For us Christians, facing death means facing life, because we know that when we die we follow in the steps of Jesus, who himself rose from death and made possible for us a new life with a renewed and glorious body. And the life we live here on earth meanwhile becomes even more precious and meaningful because it is part of that ongoing life we live in God.

From *Give Us This Day*

There is a life to live, and as we face up to death we know we follow in the steps of Jesus. He promises to sustain us and help us to find courage and hope to face the future.

WORDS OF HOPE AND FAITH

John 8: 25–32

'Who are you?' they asked.

'Just what I have been claiming all along,' Jesus replied. 'I have much to say in judgment of you. But he who sent me is reliable, and what I have heard from him I tell the world.'

They did not understand that he was telling them about his Father. So Jesus said, 'When you have lifted up the Son of Man, then you will know that I am the one I claim to be and that I do nothing on my own but speak just what the Father has taught me. The one who sent me is with me; he has not left me alone, for I always do what pleases him.' Even as he spoke, many put their faith in him.

To the Jews who had believed him, Jesus said, 'If you hold to my teaching, you are really my disciples. Then you will know the truth, and the truth will set you free.'

'Then you will know the truth, and the truth will set you free' (John 8:32). This verse is the foundation on which all my counselling rests. I am privileged to accompany my clients on their inner journey of reclaiming the wounded parts of themselves. As they face these hidden truths, so they find freedom to value and have confidence in who they really are.

> *Give sorrow words; the grief that does not speak*
> *Whispers the oe'r-fraught heart and bids it break.*

> (*Macbeth*, Act IV, Scene III)

Allowing the pain of loss to be 'spoken' (i.e. to be known) is the surest way through the valley of bereavement. Shakespeare highlights so well the vulnerability of the broken heart and the path to restoration.

In addition to those lines by Shakespeare I have chosen two poems. First, Dylan Thomas's fierce poem illustrates an angry, passionate love that wants to stand between life and death. He rages against the inevitable hand of death to which all must bow.

> *Do not go gentle into that good night,*
> *Old age should burn and rave at close of day;*
> *Rage, rage against the dying of the light.*

> *Though wise men at their end know dark is right,*
> *Because their words had forked no lightning they*
> *Do not go gentle into that good night.*

> *Good men, the last wave by, crying how bright*
> *Their frail deeds might have danced in a green bay,*
> *Rage, rage against the dying of the light.*

Wild men who caught and sang the sun in flight,
And learn, too late, they grieved it on its way,
Do not go gentle into that good night.

Grave men, near death, who see with blinding sight
Blind eyes could blaze like meteors and be gay,
Rage, rage against the dying of the light.

And you, my father, there on the sad height,
Curse, bless, me now with your fierce tears, I pray.
Do not go gentle into that good night.
Rage, rage against the dying of the light.

Dylan Thomas, 1914–53

In addition I have chosen a sonnet by John Donne – mainly because I love John Donne! In this sonnet he cocks a snook at death, which must give way before the towering presence of Christ. 'Death, thou shalt die.'

Death be not proud, though some have callèd thee
Mighty and dreadfull, for, thou art not soe,
For those whom thou think'st thou dost overthrow
Die not, poore Death, nor yet canst thou kill mee;
From rest and sleepe, which but thy pictures bee,
Much pleasure, then from thee, much more must flow,
And soonest our best men with thee doe goe,
Rest of their bones, and soules deliverie.
Thou art slave to Fate, chance, kings, and desperate men,

And dost with poyson, warre, and sicknesse dwell,
And poppie, or charmes can make us sleepe as well,
And better than thy stroake; why swell'st thou then?
One short sleepe past, wee wake eternally,
And death shall be no more. Death, thou shalt die.

John Donne, 1572–1631

FOR REFLECTION . . .

1 Have you suffered loss? Was this through death or one of the other causes listed on page 80, e.g. loss of job, loss of youth, financial loss . . . ?

2 Do you find the 'four stages of loss' helpful? Do you recognise them from your own experience or from the experience of someone else?

3 To whom would you turn if you were in emotional turmoil – a friend, relative or neighbour, a pastor, a counsellor . . . ?

4 A passage often used at funerals is the Victorian Henry Scott Holland's, 'Death is nothing at all'. Your loved ones live on; it's as though they were in the next room, says that writer. This is very different from the response of Dylan Thomas and Stephen's friends (page 88 and 93). Does Henry Scott Holland present true or false comfort, in your view?

5 Do you ever think about your own death? Do you find comfort in your faith? Or do you feel that your faith is inadequate – or even absent? If

so, can you think of someone with whom you can share this?

5

Living with depression: John's story

John Young was born in Middlesex and has had a number of jobs – paperboy, hospital porter, factory worker, soldier and teacher. Since 1964 he has been an ordained minister in the Church of England. He has written a dozen books (see page ii) and is a co-founder of York Courses. In 1988 he was invited by the Archbishop of York to take up the new post of Diocesan Evangelist. John is married to Isabel and they have two married daughters and three grandchildren.

During my thirty-six years as a Christian minister I have met a steady stream of people suffering from depression.

I remember Susan, whose engagement was threatened by the illness, and Mark, a student who fell behind with his essays. Then there was Jim, an older man who used to go visibly white when severe depression hit him, and Mary, who made more than one attempt to 'end it all'.

I think, too, of a senior church leader who sometimes had to cancel speaking engagements at short notice. And I recall Margaret, whose three children had a rota of families they would ring with a standard request: 'Mum is in bed today. Could you collect us, please?'

Over the years I came to have enormous respect for many people who wrestled with this aggressive and persistent giant. From their experience I learned how debilitating and widespread it is. So I was not surprised to discover that around 30 per cent of people in Britain suffer occasional bouts of depression. Real depression, that is, not just feeling 'down'.

People in depression often feel that they are in a dark tunnel which will go on for ever. In fact, most of them will emerge into the sunshine after a few weeks or months. For a smaller number, this particular form of mental illness may mean hospitalisation and coming to terms with permanent medication.

As a result of my pastoral work I had privileged insights into this debilitating illness but I had no personal experience 'from the inside'. Not, that is, until I was in my mid-fifties . . .

I had always enjoyed robust good health and high energy levels. Friends and family sometimes warned me that I was overdoing it, but it wasn't easy to get off the roundabout of activity.

My work as Diocesan Evangelist was varied and

interesting. I worked with individuals and small groups, preached in numerous churches of every denomination and tradition, wrote courses and books, and undertook quite a lot of radio work.

Occasionally I was privileged to interview well-known personalities in front of a thousand or more people. These included Lord Tonypandy, the Archbishops of Canterbury and York, Roy and Fiona Castle, Dame Cicely Saunders and Jonathan Edwards (and more recently, Lisa Potts GM). I enjoyed every aspect of my work and moved from one activity to another with hardly a pause for breath.

Then I came to realise that I was running out of steam. I had less enthusiasm for my work and less energy with which to do it. One morning, I woke up but did not want to get up. Half past seven ticked on to half past eight, and half past eight ticked on to ten. At noon my conscience got the better of me and I dragged myself out of bed. I seemed to have a lead ball – heavy and grey – growing in my stomach, and every small task seemed to be a mountain which had to be climbed. I was suffering from depression.

After that, each morning was the same. I struggled with an almost overwhelming desire to remain in bed, where I didn't have to do anything or make any decisions. The lead ball seemed to grow in size. By doing the minimum, I managed to scrape by. But I knew that I couldn't carry on like this much longer.

One factor was in my favour. I had cleverly timed my illness to coincide with Wimbledon fortnight! At the same time I discovered a wonderful, leisurely novel by Vikram

Seth, entitled *A Suitable Boy*. The only decision that I was happy to make was whether to sit in the garden and read, or go inside and watch Wimbledon on television!

I visited an elderly friend, a retired GP. 'Should I go to the doctor?' I asked. 'If you do, he will put you on medication,' was the response. 'Do you really want that?' I didn't, but I had to do something to dissolve the lead ball, so a few days later I made an appointment. My GP was helpful, and he gave me the inevitable prescription. I sensed that taking the first tablet was a kind of Rubicon to be crossed, but I also knew that anything was better than this terrible feeling deep down inside me.

Gentle exercise was helpful so I tried to walk a mile or two every day. But sleep was the one 'activity' which brought release. When I eventually got up I looked longingly at the bed and counted the hours until I would be horizontal again.

One writer has suggested that depression is contagious. By this he means that it affects every family and workplace which includes a sufferer. Certainly I knew that my wife was worried by this sudden change in behaviour. She was very supportive but obviously felt powerless, for she had no magic wand.

As I look back I realise that I felt shame and embarrassment. When I rang to cancel or rearrange an appointment I would say that I was unwell. I would admit that I had run out of energy. Then I would go on to say that perhaps I was suffering from ME (now dignified with the longer title of Chronic Fatigue Syndrome). I half believed what I was saying and rather hoped that this would be the case. ME sounded infinitely preferable to the dreaded 'D' word.

The drugs seemed to take for ever to do their work, and in the end I took myself off them, suspecting that they made me feel even more tired. This may well have been an unwise course of action, and I am not recommending it to others, simply recording what happened.

One morning I woke up to find a slight lift in my feelings. Not quite a feeling of joy, but almost. It was the beginning of the end of the dark tunnel. The lead ball began to shrink and I began to experience emotions at the other end of the spectrum. Quite soon I was back into my usual busy lifestyle. But I was left with some outstanding questions. In particular, there was the question of honesty. Was I willing to face the truth about myself, and was I willing to allow others in on the truth?

Shortly after, I watched a television series on BBC2 entitled *States of Mind*. It was a great help. The series consisted of a number of interviews between the psychiatrist Professor Anthony Clare and well-known and successful 'personalities'. These included Stephanie Cole, Imogen Stubbs and Mike Yarwood, who described their various demons, fears and triumphs. They had wrestled with a range of giants: panic attacks, phobias, alcoholism, post-traumatic stress. I was particularly interested to hear from Ludovic Kennedy, a life-long sufferer from depression. In the course of this interview I was surprised to hear Professor Clare describe depression as 'perhaps the most debilitating form of mental illness'.

These people spoke openly about their problems and I found this very helpful – and very challenging. Their openness had helped me; perhaps my openness might help others.

It was for this reason that I decided to write an article on my personal experience of depression, which I sent to the *Church Times*. They published the piece and a number of people responded. Most of these had experienced depression (either personally or in a family member or close friend) and thanked me for my 'courage'. If only they had known what a struggle I had to get to that point, and how closely I had covered my tracks for several months!

A year later the lead ball came back, uninvited and unwelcome. Once again mornings were a struggle and days were joyless. Nights – and sleep – came as the only release. This notion of sleep as a means of escape is why depression is such a dangerous illness. It is not for nothing that death is sometimes referred to as 'the big sleep'.

I love life and have never given a thought to ending it. During my period of depression, suicide didn't become a big issue for me, but I do recall sitting in a traffic jam and looking longingly at the exhaust pipe in front of me.

This gave me a tiny glimpse into the frame of mind which drives people to suicide – the desperate desire to end it all and to escape from the oppressive, life-draining darkness. Not, I suspect, to escape from the circumstances of their lives, however desperate and tangled they might be. Rather, the need to escape from the depression itself. From the greyness, the weight pressing down, the lead ball within, or whatever the image may be for them.

The most dangerous time, it seems, is when the sufferer is getting better. In deep depression, they lack the mental energy to make plans and the physical energy to put plans into action. But as the depression lifts, energy returns and 'never again' can become very attractive.

The same downward spiral took place. Letters went unopened, phone calls took a tremendous effort and the prospect of standing up in front of a group of people was too daunting to contemplate.

This time my hesitation was short-lived and I went back to my GP within a week. Once again he prescribed medication – a different formula which seemed to have fewer side-effects (by which I mean that I felt rather less drowsy in the mornings).

In the middle of all this I attended a conference – not as a speaker, but as a delegate. A kindly friend carried my case up the two flights of stairs to my room. 'Help, I have no energy' seemed to be stamped on my forehead.

I opted out of most of the conference sessions. Usually I get a buzz from these annual gatherings of missioners and evangelists. The speakers are stimulating, the exchange of views is lively and the Christian fellowship is warm. This year it was different. I took a few walks, and went swimming once, but most of the time I sat in my room, reading yet another long novel. It was very helpful to escape in my imagination to another world and enter into other lives.

That conference proved a perfect place of retreat and

quiet. The phone did not ring (no mobile phone for me!), letters did not arrive, and all decisions were on hold. All decisions, that is, except one. For at that conference I made one of my biggest decisions ever. I decided to take early retirement. In fact, the phrase 'I decided' is not really appropriate, for the decision took itself.

At mealtimes I looked around at my lively, able colleagues. I made myself enter into the banter, for I didn't want to be a party pooper. And I felt an enormous sense of relief. The Church would carry on perfectly well without my tiny contribution. Indeed, it became clear to me that by holding on to my post I was blocking the way for someone more able, more energetic and much more effective.

The thought of a leisurely, unpressurised life was very attractive and the anticipation made me feel better. I thought of the assertion of the remarkable French intellectual Simone Weil: 'The most beautiful life possible has always seemed to me to be one where everything is determined, either by the pressure of circumstances or by impulses . . . and where there is never any room for choice' (*Waiting on God*, Collins, 1951).

I shared all this with a friend, who said, 'You may be right. But please don't make that decision until you've recovered fully, and are back in the hurly burly of your normal life.'

He was right. As I look back I believe that after those two bouts of depression, I entered one of the most creative periods of my life.

All that was seven years ago and the depression has not returned. Since then I have written two of the longest and most demanding of my dozen books (*Teach Yourself Christianity* and *Explore Your Faith*: both paperbacks published by Hodder and Stoughton; see page ii for a full list), founded (with my colleague Simon Stanley) *York Courses*, providing audio-tape courses used by tens of thousands each year, presented several radio programmes, helped to launch an ecumenical youth trust and helped to organise several significant conferences and events (significant in my view, at least!). Also, I have preached, talked and interviewed in numerous churches and secular venues.

All this will, I hope, be a great encouragement to some readers. There *is* life after depression, however long and dark the tunnel may seem. Having said that, I would stress that my experience is, well . . . *my* experience.

It is by no means unique, and several of the 30 per cent of the population who grapple with this giant from time to time will echo some, at least, of what I have tried to express. But I am conscious that I have got off very lightly. We need to remember that smaller number for whom depression is not a giant but a monster: those who need treatment in hospital, and those who seldom emerge into the sunshine.

Where does depression come from? Sometimes the causes are clear. Loss, perhaps. Or deep disappointment, or frustration. A disastrous decision, maybe. Exhaustion and overwork. Money worries. Abuse in childhood. Or an important relationship which turns sour.

Sometimes, of course, we simply cannot discern a reason. It comes unheralded, from the deep recesses of our lives, where it has been waiting, lurking, barely awake.

When asked to describe their experience, people use a range of images. A tidal wave engulfing them, a heavy weight pressing down, endless darkness or greyness, walking through treacle, a ball of lead in the stomach (my own experience) or Winston Churchill's famous 'black dog'.

What took me completely by surprise was just how *physical* it was. Depression may be a mental illness but it affects the body, causing inertia and deep weariness.

Throughout Christian history, believers have talked about 'the dark night of the soul'. Perhaps the best way of understanding this is to explore its opposite. The brilliant mathematician and devout seventeenth-century Christian Blaise Pascal experienced what he called his 'night of fire'. In his *Pensées* he wrote: 'Fire . . . Certainty . . . Peace . . . Joy, tears of joy'.

On that occasion he had a profound sense of the presence of God, and an overwhelming assurance of the reality of the Divine. Hence his famous statement that 'the heart has its reasons, of which reason knows nothing'.

In contrast, 'the dark night of the soul' is an experience of desolation and (sometimes) doubt. God seems distant, if not absent. This was not my experience. Throughout my weeks of depression I did not doubt the reality of God, even though prayer proved difficult. Indeed, I was (rightly, I think) content to use a few 'formal' prayers. Other people expressed things better than I could, and I was grateful that they had written down the desires of their hearts, in words which I could make my own.

And I was grateful for those who prayed for me. I felt like the man carried to Jesus on a stretcher by four friends. Jesus healed the man, 'on seeing their faith'. Was that the faith of four or five men? I'm not sure. But I do know that I was buoyed up and encouraged by the prayers – and the good listening – of a few trusted friends.

On 13 February 2000, the BBC invited me to lead a morning service on Radio 4. The theme was 'Depression' and I'll end by quoting some extracts from that service.

* * *

Do not withhold your mercy from me, O LORD;
    may your love and your truth always protect me.
For troubles without number surround me;
    my sins have overtaken me, and I cannot see.
They are more than the hairs of my head,
    and my heart fails within me.

(Psalm 40:11–12)

These verses from one of the 'troubled psalms' raise an important question. Christians sometimes feel guilty about depression. Surely this is a failure of faith? What do the Scriptures say about that?

The Bible announces 'glad tidings of great joy' with its emphasis on resurrection, the love of God, new life in Christ and glory to come. But it caters for all moods and conditions, and there is another side. Indeed, the Scriptures contain quite a lot of material about, and by, people suffering from depression. The fiery prophet Elijah, for example. Having triumphed fearlessly over a host of prophets of Baal, he ran away in fear and eventually lay down utterly exhausted, longing only for the release of death. This gives rise to the gentle, moving story of the way in which God met his physical needs.

In 1 Kings 19:4 we read that Elijah 'came to a broom tree, sat down under it and prayed that he might die'. Several Bible passages speak the same language of bewilderment and distress – which often gives way to quiet faith or triumphant praise.

Psalm 13, for example, starts in desolation but ends with praise: 'How long will you hide your face from me? How long must I wrestle with my thoughts and every day have sorrow in my heart . . . But I trust in your unfailing love; my heart rejoices in your salvation.'

The New Testament also brings encouragement to those wrestling with depression, for it shows with great honesty the way in which some of its leading figures grappled with despair and darkness. The best-known example is Jesus in the Garden of Gethsemane – perhaps the most solemn episode in the entire Gospel story. That whole passage is heavy with dread and desolation: 'My soul is overwhelmed with sorrow . . . *Abba*, Father, take this cup from me. Yet not what I will but what you will.'

Significantly, the whole mood stands in surprising and stark contrast to the way in which the early martyrs faced death. The female slave Blandina, for example, who, reported Eusebius, went to her death in 177 AD as to a marriage feast. Or Polycarp, Bishop of Smyrna, who as an old man stood in a pagan arena in 156 AD. He was offered his life in exchange for denying Christ, to which he answered, 'I have been his servant for eighty-six years and he has never done me any wrong. How then can I blaspheme my king, who saved me?' He was burned to death.

Neither Blandina nor Polycarp showed dread in the face of death. Indeed, both drew strength from their faith in Jesus Christ, despite the fact that *he* shrank from the cross. In pondering this great mystery, theologians have found a profound answer. Jesus shrank from death for he was, in the words of John the Baptist, 'the Lamb of God who takes away the sin of the world'. In doing this, he suffered spiritual suffocation – a unique and terrible experience, which set his followers free from fear and filled them with hope and faith.

Another example of faith facing depression can be found in the second letter to the Corinthians. St Paul is trying to establish his credentials as a leader and an apostle. He is remarkably frank. For he speaks not only of victory and triumph but of 'fightings without and fears within' – taking an enormous risk in exposing his vulnerability to a church which seemed to want strength, buoyancy and charisma in its leaders.

That letter contains one of the most beautiful anti-climaxes in all literature. Paul speaks about his troubles and his inner turmoil and goes on to say that 'God, who comforts the downcast, comforted us' (2 Corinthians 7:6).

From the New Testament we know a fair bit about the life of St Paul. So we might expect him to go on to say that God comforted him by a dream, a vision or an in-filling of the Holy Spirit. Something dramatic. In fact he completes his sentence rather lamely: 'But God, who comforts the downcast, comforted us by the coming of Titus.' His friend turned up, bringing good news from the other churches, and this was a turning point for the apostle.

Like Paul the apostle, from my two periods of depression I discovered afresh the importance of friendship and good listening. I'm grateful to God for those who let me set the pace and who, in today's jargon, 'were there for me'.

And so to the most difficult question of all. Why does God allow such apparently unproductive suffering? The ministry of Jesus is full of healing miracles – sometimes for people whose faith was no bigger than a mustard seed. I don't doubt that the same Lord heals people today. Perhaps it is the prayers of my friends which have kept my own depression at bay.

But the New Testament outlines other experiences too. Some of the most famous prayers have been answered with a clear 'No'. We have already considered Jesus in Gethsemane. We turn now to Paul's persistent prayer for the removal of his 'thorn in the flesh'. We can't be sure what that was. Eye problems perhaps. Epilepsy maybe. Or depression. Who knows?

What we do know for certain is that Paul longed to be rid of it. It blighted his life and hindered his ministry. Try travelling vast distances in modern Turkey (his Asia Minor) on foot or pony and you'll soon see that you need to be in excellent health.

God's answer to Paul's urgent prayer was 'No'. But there was a rider. Paul needed to learn this great truth: 'My grace is sufficient for you, for my power is made perfect in weakness' (2 Corinthians 12:9).

At the heart of the Christian faith are two great miracles: incarnation and resurrection.

The incarnation is caught wonderfully by St John: 'The Word was made flesh and dwelt among us . . . full of grace and truth' (John 1:14, KJV). Jesus came among us as one of us – and he suffered for us and for our salvation. It is not surprising, therefore, that Jesus calls his followers to identify closely with a world in anguish. So – hard as it is – I believe that he calls members of his Church to suffer the full range of human miseries – from unemployment to bereavement, from cancer to depression.

It is a tough message. But when it is heard in humble obedience it can be wonderfully inspiring. Here, for example, is an extract from a letter from a friend, a deputy head, who learned that she had multiple sclerosis.

I've had to give up driving. The fatigue is rotten, but not such a worry now that I've stopped working. The blurred and double/triple vision is a nuisance, but curiously interesting. For example, the Cathedral has had two spires for a couple of years; there are three moons in the sky and an awful lot of eight-legged cats about! I am quite used to it now and it's not a worry. I've made no retirement plans, confident that something will emerge for me, when the time is right.

I think too of a conversation with a mother, following the death of her child. She told me that a particular Bible verse brought her great comfort. 'Which one?' I asked, expecting her to quote from the resurrection narratives. 'The words of Jesus on the cross,' she replied. ' "My God, my God, why have you forsaken me?" ' She drew strength from the knowledge that Jesus was with her in her sorrow – and that he understood and shared her desolation.

And so we end with a hymn by Charles Wesley, which catches and mingles the twin themes of confidence in the love of God and realism about the storms of life. Verse 2 reads like this:

> *Other refuge have I none,*
> *Hangs my helpless soul on thee;*
> *Leave, ah, leave me not alone,*
> *Still support and comfort me.*
> *All my trust on thee is stayed,*
> *All my help from thee I bring;*
> *Cover my defenceless head*
> *With the shadow of thy wing.*

WORDS OF HOPE AND FAITH

From the Bible I have selected 2 Corinthians 7:2–7, for the reasons set out on pages 109–10.

2 Corinthians 7:2–7

Make room for us in your hearts. We have wronged no-one, we have corrupted no-one, we have exploited no-one. I do not say this to condemn you; I have said before that you have such a place in our hearts that we would live or die with you.

I have great confidence in you; I take great pride in you. I am greatly encouraged; in all our troubles my joy knows no bounds.

For when we came into Macedonia, this body of ours had no rest, but we were harassed at every turn – conflicts on the outside, fears within. But God, who comforts the downcast, comforted us by the coming of Titus, and not only by his coming but also by the comfort you had given him. He told us about your longing for me, your deep sorrow, your ardent concern for me, so that my joy was greater than ever.

In addition, I have chosen a poem by the so called 'rustic poet', John Clare, an uneducated but outstanding nine-teenth-century poet. He suffered from severe mental illness and spent the last twenty-three years of his life in the General Lunatic Asylum in Northampton. John Clare's poem catches the anguish of mental illness and the deep longing for release. Despite the bleakness of his experience, he expresses his faith in 'my Creator, God'.

> *I am: yet what I am none cares or knows*
> *My friends forsake me like a memory lost;*
> *I am the self-consumer of my woes,*
> *They rise and vanish in oblivious host,*
> *Like shades in love and death's oblivion lost;*
> *And yet I am, and live with shadows lost.*
>
> *Into the nothingness of scorn and noise,*
> *Into the living sea of waking dreams,*
> *Where there is neither sense of life nor joys,*
> *But the vast shipwreck of my life's esteems;*
> *And e'en the dearest — that I loved the best —*
> *Are strange — nay, rather stranger than the rest.*
>
> *I long for scenes where man has never trod,*
> *A place where woman never smiled or wept;*
> *There to abide with my Creator, God,*
> *And sleep as I in childhood sweetly slept;*
> *Untroubling and untroubled where I lie,*
> *The grass below — above the vaulted sky.*

John Clare, 1793–1864

I have also chosen two paragraphs from Roman Catholic writers. The former Archbishop of Liverpool, Derek Worlock, wrote with stark insight about his own emotional 'deadness' as he wrestled with the giant of terminal lung cancer.

> *I remained cold as a stone spiritually and desperately troubled by nightmares ... Our own sufferings and difficulties can seem cruel and pointless unless they are related to the work of salvation. In our hearts we know that properly directed, they can be a way in which we are drawn into the life and purpose of our Saviour. That is never easy for us but it is part of our faith.*

> From *With Hope in Our Hearts*
> (Hodder and Stoughton, 1994)

Following Derek Worlock's testimony we read a gentler piece by Basil Hume. The late Cardinal wrote about 'friendship with God'. This concept is vitally important, but always stands in danger of sounding sentimental. As we reflect on Basil Hume's own heroic and inspiring battle with terminal cancer, we see just how sustaining a deep but simple faith in the God who invites our friendship can be.

> *Holiness involves friendship with God. God's love for us and ours for him grows like any relationship with other people. There comes a moment, which we can never quite locate or catch, when an acquaintance becomes a friend. In a sense, the change from one to the other has been taking place over a period of time, but there comes a point when*

we know we can trust the other, exchange confidences, keep each other's secrets. We are friends. There has to be a moment like that in our relationship with God. He ceases to be just a Sunday acquaintance and becomes a weekday friend.

From *To Be a Pilgrim* (SPCK, 1984)

FOR REFLECTION . . .

1   Do you know people who have suffered from depression? Are you a sufferer? Re-read the list of images on page 106 used to describe depression. What do you make of these 'pictures'? Do you want to add to that list?

2   Describe your reaction to those who suffer from depression: concern, helplessness, pity, irritation . . . If you were totally honest with them, what would you say?

3   If you suffer from depression, what – if you dared – would you most like to say to your family, friends and colleagues about the way they treat you?

4   'Snap out of it.' We are all aware of the inadequacy and foolishness of such a comment. But might there be *some* truth in it – after all, many people who suffer from depression do seem to develop strategies for coping.

5   The giants which you know well may not be described in these chapters. There are many others. Draw up a list and identify those with which you, and those close to you, struggle. Does your faith help? How?

York Courses

John Young and Simon Stanley founded *York Courses* in 1997. They have produced a number of **Topic Tapes** in addition to those outlined on page 3 on which this book is based:

- a sixty-minute conversation on '**Science and Christian Faith**' with Rev. Professor John Polkinghorne FRS, former Cambridge Professor of Mathematical Physics
- two tapes on '**Evangelism**' with Rev. Robin Gamble, Rev. Brian Hoare, Bishop Gavin Reid and Canon Robert Warren
- a twenty-minute tape entitled '**Finding Faith**'. It contains four personal journeys into faith (including that of the Archbishop of York), Bible readings and prayers.

In addition to the Topic Tapes, there is a series of **audio tapes for group discussion**, together with accompanying notes/booklets. Contributors to these courses include: Paul Boateng MP, Fiona Castle, Steve Chalke, Father Gerard Hughes SJ, Bishop David Konstant, Rev. Dr Tom Wright, Professor Frances Young and the Most Rev. and Rt. Hon. David Hope.

Further details on all these courses are available from:

York Courses
St Barnabas Vicarage
PO Box 3343, York YO19 5YB

Tel: 01904 481677
E-mail: yorkcourses©barn.clara.net

Also by John Young

The Case Against Christ

In this bestselling book, John Young acts as counsel for the defence in the case against Christ and invites atheists, agnostics and enquirers to join the lively debate. Material for group discussion is also included.

'*A Classic*.' CHURCH PASTORAL AID SOCIETY

'*If ministers will put this book to use among all the members of their congregations, the result will be many less defensive Christians, better able to cope with the usual charges against their position*.'
CHURCH OF ENGLAND NEWSPAPER

'*Quite first class*.' BISHOP HUGH MONTEFIORE

Hodder & Stoughton
ISBN 0 340 52462 6

Explore Your Faith

Eight study courses for groups and individual readers. Courses include the teaching of Jesus, evangelism without an evangelist, foundations for Christian living and a course on 'listening'.

Most of these courses are linked with a *York Course* which includes contributions from: Poal Boateng MP, Fiona Castle, Steve Chalke, Father Gerard Hughes SJ, Bishop David Konstant, Rev. Dr Tom Wright, Professor Frances Young and the Most Rev. and Rt Hon. David Hope.

Hodder & Stoughton
ISBN 0 340 73540 6

Know Your Faith

The excitement of Christian truth presented afresh in an eight-week study of the Apostles' Creed. This book is designed for individual readers and for discussion groups.

'*A major resource.*' GEORGE CAREY,
THE ARCHBISHOP OF CANTERBURY

'*John Young has a great gift for communicating profound ideas simply and readably.*'
JOHN HABGOOD, FORMER ARCHBISHOP OF YORK

'*An excellent course.*' BRIAN HOARE,
PAST PRESIDENT OF THE METHODIST CONFERENCE

Hodder & Stoughton
ISBN 0 340 54487 2

Teach Yourself Christianity

An introduction to Christianity as a living faith in the renowned *Teach Yourself* series. A rich resource which ranges from the Toronto Blessing to Transubstantiation, and from Jesus, prayer and the Christian experience of God to Christianity in a scientific age and significant modern movements within the Church.

'*It not only informs, it excites.*' DAVID HOPE,
ARCHBISHOP OF YORK

'*. . . this important book.*' JAMES JONES,
BISHOP OF LIVERPOOL

'*An amazing compilation.*' DR PETER BRIERLEY,
CHRISTIAN RESEARCH

Hodder & Stoughton
ISBN 0 340 77256 5